Simplifying
sugar flowers

Simplifying
sugar flowers

Alison Procter

Contents

Introduction

The aim of this book is to help newcomers to the art of making sugar flowers achieve pleasing results right from the beginning, by simplifying the techniques involved. It should also assist those who have been decorating cakes for some time, by opening up all kinds of possibilities for making flowers that have previously seemed unachievable.

It was never my intention that every flower and leaf should be copied exactly – use my examples as starting points, and then allow your own ideas to unfold. Learn to think shape not flower, and you will soon discover that there are only a few basic shapes, but thousands of flowers to be made!

In addition, I have offered some new ideas on making up the finished flower arrangements and presenting them on cakes in a range of shapes and sizes, which should make this whole process a lot easier and the finished results more successful. Again, no fixed quantities are specified for the flowers used – it's up to you. Just remember to use plenty of leaves, as the various greens provide a backdrop that makes the colours of the flowers appear more vibrant.

Working in these ways, my sugarcraft has helped me to understand and study the flowers I paint in watercolour and oils. I hope you will enjoy making the flowers in this book as much as I have, and that the ideas demonstrated here will prove a springboard to many more exciting projects of your own.

Dedication

This book is dedicated to Tony, my ever-patient and supportive husband, and to my family, especially my grandchildren Emma, Oliver, and Benjamin.

To Lisa Procter, my grateful thanks – without your computer skills I would have found writing this book very difficult indeed.

Equipment, techniques and recipes

The basic equipment needed for making the flowers in this book is listed here and these items are not repeated for each flower project. However, any special equipment required for making a particular flower is listed with the instructions for that flower.

EQUIPMENT
CUTTING BOARD
Choose a purpose-made polypropylene board. Before use, prime it with a little *fresh* vegetable fat rubbed on with kitchen paper.

A cutting board measuring 30x24cm (12x9½in) is the most useful size.

If you are right-handed, keep an area on the right-hand side of the board that you grease each time you work a shape. Always position the board at the edge of the table, and your work at the edge of the board.

I rarely use cornflour on my board or tools. Where used, this is specified in the instructions for the projects.

Make sure that you wash your board regularly in hot, soapy water. It may become well marked from cutting out flowers and leaves, but unless the surface is deeply scored this will not matter. In fact, I prefer a well-used board – a new, shiny board tends to be more of a hazard than a help.

Bind the florist's tape with tension so that it will remain in place.

WIRES
The gauge and colour of wire required for making the flowers is listed in the individual projects. I generally use white for petals and green for leaves and stems.

However, not all plant stems are green. There are many different-coloured wires on the market, but they are usually 26-gauge. To produce a specific colour for a project, put a drop of the appropriate droplet colour (see page 10) on a plate and add drops of water until the desired colour is achieved. Pull white

wires through the diluted liquid, holding them down with a damp sponge. Immediately place the wires on kitchen paper to dry.

Alternatively, place some dusting powder – especially glitter powder – on a wet wipe, fold over the paper and then pull a white wire through.

To hook a wire, bend over one end by about 2.5mm (⅛in) with tweezers.

FLORIST'S TAPE
Florist's stretch paper tape is used for making all the flowers in this book. If you use a tape cutter, clean the blades

EQUIPMENT AND MATERIALS
1 Dusting powders
2 Palette
3 Serrator
4 Wire cutters
5 Scissors
6 Leaf aid tool
7 Tweezers
8 Leicester tool
9 Palette knife
10 Paintbrush
11 Craft knife
12 Dogbone tool
13 Florist's tape
14 Cocktail sticks
15 Selection of cutters
16 Flower pad
17 Rolling pin

frequently. The tape will blunt the blades, so change them regularly.

White tape can be coloured to a specific shade to make coloured bracts, stamen heads and so on. Place a length of full-width white tape on kitchen paper and dip a make-up sponge into the appropriate dusting powder (see page 10), then brush the tape vigorously on both sides. Then cut, if necessary, to the correct width.

FLOWERPASTE (GUM PASTE)
The recipe for the flowerpaste used to make the flowers and leaves in this book is provided on page 11.

Keep flowerpaste in small amounts of deep colours. When you need it, use a small quantity to colour fresh paste by kneading together.

For secondary colours such as violet or peach, mix two already coloured pastes together (blue and pink, or yellow and pink in these examples). Working in this way means that the colours are easier to repeat, and a better result is achieved.

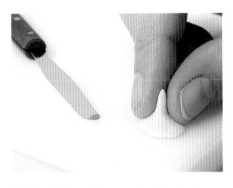

Work with small amounts of paste to form the shape that you want.

Work with a small amount of paste at a time and keep the remainder (and any paste pieces already worked) covered to prevent drying out.

After a lot of working, if the paste starts to become a little stiff, try adding a drop of water.

Go through your small packets of flowerpaste at least once a week and knead them. Any paste that has become slimy or hard can be thrown out as it will be impossible to use.

Once you have opened a new packet of flowerpaste, take great care always to keep it double wrapped in plastic when not in use.

CUTTERS (see pages 124–5)
The instructions for individual flower projects each specify the

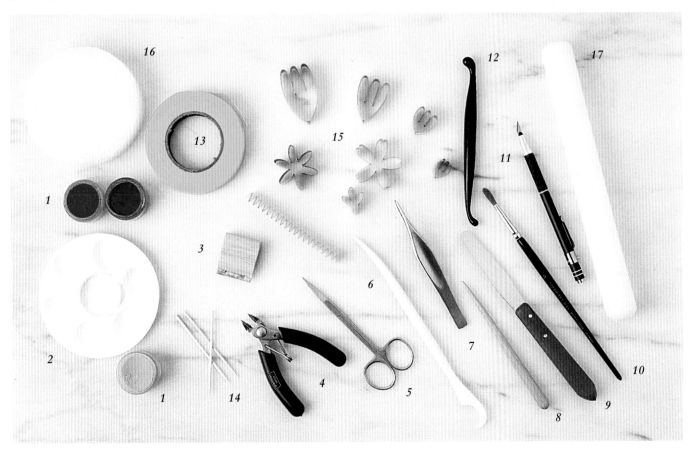

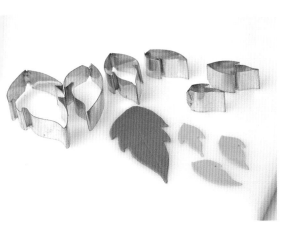

Flower, petal and leaf cutters come in a range of different sizes. In this book, most cutters are used to make more than one flower.

cutter(s) needed to make that flower. If you do not have that particular cutter, you can use the illustration as a template (see pages 124–5): simply trace it onto a piece of lightweight card, cut out the shape and place it on the paste, then cut out around it with the tip of a sharp knife or small pair of scissors. A few of the flowers do not require a cutter.

Always make sure the paste will come off the board before you cut out. Try to take the cutter off the board with the paste in it, then brush it against the heel of your hand to give you a clean shape without any rough edges.

NOTEBOOK
It is a good idea to keep a record of plant shapes and colours in a notebook, by either writing notes or drawing a detailed diagram (or both). The real thing never seems to be available when you need to copy it, so make sure you jot down details when the opportunity arises.

TOOLS
A selection of the following tools is used when making most of the flowers in this book.

COCKTAIL STICKS
These are plain wooden sticks, not to be confused with toothpicks with a carved end. To prepare these for use, cut off one end with wire cutters and then round it off with an emery board or sandpaper. Before working flowerpaste on a lightly greased board with a cocktail stick, always press it down with your index finger to make sure it sticks.

The blunt end of a cocktail stick is used to push paste into small spaces.

There are four different pressure points on a cocktail stick: the point, the shoulder, the main shaft and the blunt end. The 'shoulder' is the lowest part of the point. It is used when you want to thin just part of the petal. Use the blunt end when every part has to be spread.

LEAF AID TOOL
This tool is extremely useful for veining and curling petals and leaves. Rubber veiners are unnecessary in most cases, and excellent results can be achieved by using the leaf aid tool combined with paint effects.

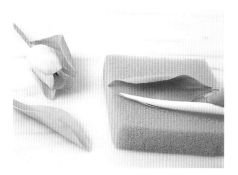

Stroke the leaf aid tool across the paste, applying very little pressure.

LEICESTER TOOL
This tapered wooden tool is very useful for rolling out areas of paste that are too small for a rolling pin but too large for a cocktail stick.

A Leicester tool will not bend, and does not slip on the paste.

DOGBONE TOOL
This tool has a large and a small rounded end, and is used for making soft curves.

Working on soft foam, pressure from the dogbone tool will curve petals.

FLOWER PAD

Push the wire of your flower into this, so that you have two hands free for working. Insert only one item at a time, to avoid damaging completed work. A circular pad is better, as it does not tip over as readily as a square or rectangular shape.

A polystyrene block is useful for holding completed flowers and leaves while they dry.

Insert the flower in the flower pad while working the next part.

FOAM

Two types of foam are used as working bases when making the flowers in this book: hard and soft. They are *not* interchangeable, so follow the project instructions carefully. Ripple foam is also used in some projects as a flower support.

Use ripple foam to help support petals while they dry.

TECHNIQUES
WORKING THE FLOWERS

Work the paste until it is pliable and stretchy before rolling out. Do not roll it out too thinly, especially where you will be working on it with a cocktail stick.

• Always try to use a cutter shape that is narrower than the finished article, even if you have to cut pieces away from certain areas at the start in order to help achieve the final shape.

• When thinning and shaping the paste, work with the shape on a lightly greased board. Treat every petal or leaf, however small or large, as two halves, working one half outwards in a fan shape before repeating for the other half.

• When working on flowers and leaves, try holding the leaf aid tool, dogbone tool, and in some instances the paintbrush, from above the shaft. If you hold them from underneath this raises the angle and can cause excessive pressure.

Use a pair of blunt tweezers to pinch the paste into the required shape.

• It is very important to get used to holding wires between your thumb and third finger. This will enable you to move the wire at a speed convenient to you while you model, pinch paste onto the wire, or remove surplus paste with your two index fingers and the thumb of the other hand. Try never to use just two fingers. It may feel very awkward to start off with, but persevere.

Place a petal on soft foam to help the curving of the edges with a leaf aid tool.

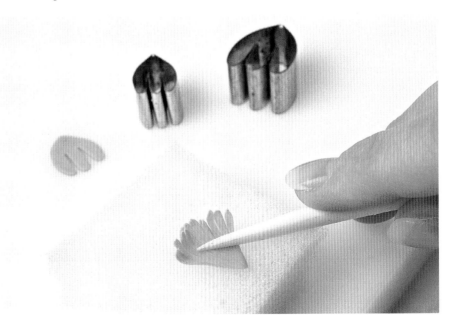

STAMENS

Multiple stamens for flowers such as open roses, anemones and clematis can be made using ordinary cotton thread. Do not use a manmade fibre, as this will not stiffen with egg white.

Make stamens from natural cotton thread in one or more colours.

1 Leaving a tail of about 8cm (3in) hanging, wind the thread around two fingers the specified number of times, and finish by leaving an 8cm (3in) tail at the opposite side of the loop. Pull the wound thread off your fingers, push a wire through the loop and then twist. Repeat at the other end. Using the free length of thread, tie twice securely near the base of the thread loops, just above the wires.

2 Using two reels together will halve the number of times you have to wind the thread around your fingers. You can also use two different shades together, such as cream and pale green for a wild rose or clematis, or cream and light brown for a fully open or spent rose.

COLOURINGS

PASTE FOOD COLOURS
These colours are used throughout the book to colour flowerpaste for leaves and some petals.

DROPLET COLOURS
These highly concentrated colours are used to colour flowerpaste, royal icing and, diluted, for staining wires.

DUSTING POWDERS
These are used to enhance the shading on flowers and leaves. A darker colour on the edge of leaves gives the impression of light filtering through the foliage.

Dusting powders can also be used to colour flowerpaste. Place a small pile of powder on a plate, mix in

Dust one shade on top of another to achieve subtle finished effects.

drops of water to form a thick paste and then work into the flowerpaste.

PAINT AID
This is a commercially prepared liquid which helps to fix powder colour. Use it when you want a velvet finish, as with pansies, anemones or petunias. You can also use it to block out underlying colour completely – for example, with the yellow marking on a dark-coloured iris, or on a yellow pansy with some petals in a darker colour.

Good sable brushes hold moisture well, but always wash after use.

PAINTBRUSHES
Dip sable brushes in hair conditioner occasionally and then rinse well. If you have lost the point on a sable brush, boil a kettle, then dip the brush quickly into the water and it may come back to a point.

RECIPES

FLOWERPASTE (GUM PASTE)

All the flowers and leaves are made with this universally useful paste. (Commercially made flowerpaste is available from all good cake decorating and sugarcraft shops.)

> 450g (1lb/4 cups) icing
> (confectioner's) sugar
> 3 level teaspoons gum tragacanth
> 2 teaspoons powdered gelatine
> 5 teaspoons warm water
> 2 teaspoons liquid glucose
> 10g (⅓oz) white vegetable fat
> (shortening)
> 1 large egg white

1 Sift the icing (confectioner's) sugar into a bowl and mix in the gum tragacanth. Warm in the oven, over a pan of hot water or in a microwave. Meanwhile, put all the remaining ingredients except the egg white into a bowl over a pan of hot water and heat until liquid. Pour the liquid into the warm sugar.

2 Warm the beater for the mixer. Transfer the sugar mixture to the mixer bowl (if not already in it). With the mixer at its lowest speed, pour in the egg white, placing a cloth over the top as the mixture starts to take up the egg white. Beat until the mixture begins to cool. As it thickens it will come away from the side of the bowl in strings.

3 Store the flowerpaste in a plastic bag inside an airtight container in the refrigerator. Leave for 24 hours before using.

GUM ARABIC SOLUTION

This is used in conjunction with Holly Leaf or Fern droplet colour to paint leaves. Place 1 part gum arabic to 3 parts triple-strength rosewater (available from good chemists) in a screw-top jar, give it a good shake and when dissolved strain into a jar with a lid.

GELATINE DROPLETS

These are used to look like dew on leaves, petals and lacework.

> 30ml (1fl oz) cold water
> 2 level teaspoons powdered gelatine

1 Pour the cold water into a small bowl, sprinkle on the gelatine and allow to 'sponge' (about 30 seconds). Place the bowl in a saucepan of warm water and heat through gently.

2 Tape part of a roasting bag securely onto a board with masking tape. When the mixture in the container becomes clear, suck up the liquid with a straight glass medicine dropper. Then release one tiny drop at a time onto the board: the action is to touch the board and lift away. Keep the pressure constant on the rubber end to avoid sucking up air. If some droplets come out with air, these will dry with the appearance of little bubbles, which can be used to look as though a drop of water has just fallen. You may need to rinse out the dropper in hot water from time to time, as the gelatine tends to solidify if allowed to cool inside the narrow dropper.

3 Leave the droplets to dry at least overnight, then scrape them off the surface with a palette knife. Handle the droplets with tweezers – you will not break them. Attach to the leaf or petal with dots of royal icing, or dip into egg white and then stick onto the leaf or petal edge or surface. Store in a small container. Gelatine droplets will keep almost indefinitely.

SUGARPASTE (ROLLED FONDANT)

This paste is used as the top covering on a cake that has been covered with marzipan or buttercream.

> 1 egg white, made up from dried
> egg albumen
> 2 tablespoons liquid glucose
> 575g (1¼lb/5 cups) icing
> (confectioner's) sugar
> A little white vegetable fat (shortening),
> if required

1 Put the egg white and liquid glucose into a bowl using a warm spoon for the glucose.

2 Sift the icing (confectioner's) sugar into the bowl, adding a little at a time and stirring until thickened.

3 Turn out onto a work surface dusted with icing sugar and knead the paste until it is soft, smooth and pliable. If the paste is dry and cracked, fold in a little vegetable fat (shortening) and knead again.

4 Put the paste into a plastic bag, or double wrap it in cling film (plastic wrap), and then store in an airtight container.

flowers

Anemone

Cutter Nos 9 (six or eight points),
   32 and 37

White (or just off-white) flowerpaste
   (gum paste) for flowers and buds,
   coloured with black droplet colour
   for stamens, Christmas Green paste
   food colour for leaves

28- and 24-gauge green wires

30-gauge white wire

Nile green florist's tape

Pipe cleaners

Very pale pink or cream cotton thread
   (not manmade fibre)

Copper (optional) and range of
   appropriate colours such as Peony
   Rose, Garnette, Ruby, African Violet
   and Empress Purple dusting powders

Heraldic Black and Fern droplet colours

Paint Aid

Gum arabic solution

Rose wire

Soft foam

Ripple foam

Use these colourful flowers as an excuse to create some wonderfully vibrant displays. It is unlikely that you will need any other flowers to enhance the effect, although you could add some extra greenery to the arrangement.

STAMENS

1 Make the stamens following the instructions on page 10, winding the thread around your fingers about 60 times and using two 5cm (2in) lengths of 30-gauge white wire. Tape the stamens plus twisted wires to 24–gauge green wires (two for each stem). Tape a few extra turns around the base of the stamens to keep them firmly upright. Dip the threads in egg white and allow to dry overnight.

2 When dry, pull the stiffened threads downwards using tweezers, curving them firmly. Use a paintbrush to touch the ends of the stamens with black colour and immediately blot with kitchen paper (to prevent the colour running too far down the threads). Form a small ball of purple-black flowerpaste (gum paste), big enough to go in the centre of the stamens, and rough up the top surface with tweezers. Paint some egg white into the centre of the stamens and then put the centre in place. If necessary, tape a 5cm (2in) hooked length of rose wire to the stem so that the hook protrudes just enough to give you something with which to anchor the paste into the middle of the stamens. Bind a pipe cleaner onto the stem with full-width florist's tape now, or when the flower has dried.

FLOWER

3 Form a ball of white (or just off-white) flowerpaste about the size of a

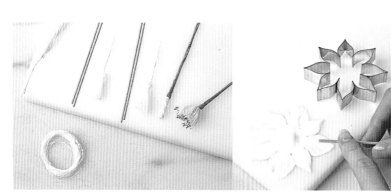

Make the stamens from cotton thread, tipped with black droplet colour.

Work the petals with a cocktail stick to change the points into a rounded shape.

Support the flower on ripple foam by pulling the wire through.

large marble. Flatten around the edges with your fingers, place on a lightly greased board and roll out reasonably thinly, leaving a very small pimple in the middle. Cut out the shape with the No. 9 cutter and, with the paste near the edge of the board and treating the petals as two halves, work on the shape with a cocktail stick to convert the points into rounded shapes. Work on alternate petals, then the remaining petals – this will ensure that some come forward and some go behind.

4 If the paste is still pliable enough, turn it over (pimple underneath) and work the edges over your index finger with the cocktail stick, so that the upper surface becomes more textured. Curve the petals on soft foam using a leaf aid tool. Make sure the pimple is in the middle – if it isn't, move it by gently rolling against it with the rolling pin. With the pimple underneath and the shape back on the board, lightly mark a continuation line from the ends of the petals to the centre with the hook of the tool.

5 Paint egg white onto the wire immediately beneath the stamens, and

quickly push the wire plus stamens through the flower shape. The wire should pass through the pimple, which is on the underside. Position the petals just below the stamens, making sure that you do not pull the stamens through too far. Immediately push the wire through ripple foam, and pull it through until the petals are resting gently on the foam. Arrange them carefully, remembering that the paste may be quite fragile by this time. Leave the flower to stand in this support, preferably overnight.

BUDS
6 Tape together two 8cm (3in) lengths of 24-gauge green wire with half-width florist's tape and hook the end. Form a shape with white

(or just off-white) flowerpaste that is similar to a rose centre (see page 52), but with a more rounded end. Dip the hooked wire in egg white and pull it through the paste. Allow to dry thoroughly.

7 Roll out some white flowerpaste and cut out the calyx shape using the No. 32 cutter. Work the paste as for the petals in step 3. Bring two inwards and leave three out if possible. Dip the dried bud centre in egg white and then pull the wire through the calyx shape until the centre is in position. Stick two petals to the bud centre and then arrange the other three petals carefully, adding more egg white if necessary to hold them snugly upright. Bind a pipe cleaner to the bud stem with full-width tape.

LEAVES
8 Follow the instructions on page 67 and see photo (left).

COLOURING AND ASSEMBLY
9 Paint the flowers and buds using Paint Aid and dusting powder in your chosen colour. Attach the three leaves to the flower stem about 2.5cm (1in) below the flower head, but a little closer to the bud.

Paint the flowers with Paint Aid and dusting powder in an appropriate colour.

Cut out irregular V shapes from the edges of the leaf 'fingers'.

Bluebell

The pretty bluebell that grows wild in our hedgerows and woods is a far more refined and delicate plant than the more robust and coarse garden version. Do not use too deep a blue for the paste, as the flowers need to be dusted a darker colour when dry. They can be a mixture of mauves and blues.

YOU WILL NEED

No cutter required

Flowerpaste (gum paste) coloured with Royal Blue droplet colour for flowers and large buds, Christmas Green paste food colour for small buds and leaves

28- and 24-gauge green wires

30-gauge white wire

White and nile green florist's tape

African Violet and Iris or Mauve Mist dusting powders

Royal Blue and Fern droplet colours

Gum arabic solution

Fine white stamens with yellow tips, cut to about 1.5cm (⅝in) long

Sponge

Kitchen paper

Piece of card or paper

Hard foam

1 Prepare the wires and florist's tape following the instructions on pages 6–7. Use Royal Blue droplet colour to colour 4cm (1½in) lengths of 30-gauge white wire to a pale blue shade to make stems for the flowers, and Iris or Mauve Mist dusting powder to colour white florist's tape for the little bracts. Cut the tape in half lengthwise, then cut a number of 2cm (¾in) lengths to make the bracts. From each of these, cut out a V shape that is roughly half the length of the piece of tape.

FLOWERS

2 From a pea-sized piece of blue flowerpaste (gum paste) form a long, thin cone, slightly longer than the length needed for the finished flower, which is about 2.5cm (1in).

Make marks on a piece of card or paper against which to measure each cone, so that the flowers will all be the same size. Open up the point of the cone with the sharp end of a cocktail stick and hollow out about two-thirds of the length. Cut out six V shapes around the open end using sharp scissors. Roll each petal with the blunt end of a cocktail stick, holding the flower against your index finger to do this.

3 Place the flower upright on hard foam with the petals splayed out. Place the blunt end of the cocktail stick on the petal, roll it lightly towards the end, and then roll it back up the petal, increasing the pressure slightly as you go. This will make the paste curl up.

For each bract, cut a V shape in the half-width tape to roughly half its length.

Measure the length of each flower cone against the pre-marked card.

Cut out six V shapes at the pointed end of the cone using sharp scissors.

4 Dip a hooked, blue-stained wire into egg white and pull through the flower, until the hook is embedded in the paste. Insert three small stamens so that they just show below the petals. Tape a bract a little way down the wire. It can be moved up or down when you assemble the plant. Each one should eventually be positioned where a flower stem joins the main stalk.

5 When the flowers are dry, dust the stalk end with a small amount of African Violet powder, then brush with Iris or Mauve Mist down the full length of the flower as far as the curled-back petals.

BUDS

6 Make some small oval buds from green flowerpaste, and some slightly larger ones from blue paste. When these are dry, dust some of the larger tips of the green buds with Iris dusting powder. Dust the blue buds in the same way as the open flowers (see step 5).

7 Tape two or three buds together with nile green florist's tape and a

few little pieces of the prepared mauve tape to look like tiny bracts.

8 Using 24-gauge wire for the stem, tape on the open flowers, all facing the same way. You will need to keep the flower wires straight and close together until the plant is assembled, then bend the whole stem into a gentle curve and shape the flower stems so that they hang down.

LEAVES

9 (For full instructions on making and colouring leaves, see pages 62–5.) Make the leaves with 28-gauge green wires. Cut out a number of leaves freehand (see page 126), and curve the overall length slightly. When dry, paint on both sides with Fern droplet colour and gum arabic solution. Tape at least three leaves to the base of each flower stem.

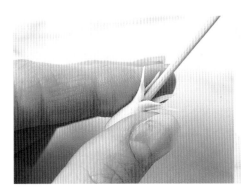

Hold the flower against your finger and thin each petal a with blunt cocktail stick.

With the flower upright, roll the petals to make them curl upwards.

Brush the flowers with dusting powder as far as the curled-back petals.

Broom

These flowers are quick to make and look very dainty. The leaves are small and narrow, and the calyx is also tiny, so rather than risk a heavy-looking paste one it is best just to paint it on. The shape used here can also be used for vetch, wisteria and other flowers.

YOU WILL NEED

Cutter No. 3

Flowerpaste (gum paste) coloured with Melon paste food colour for flowers, Christmas Green for leaves

30- and 24-gauge green wires

Nile green florist's tape

Fern droplet colour

Sunflower dusting powder

Gum arabic solution

Soft foam

FLOWERS

1 Cut 8cm (3in) lengths of 30-gauge green wire and hook one end. Take a small piece of pale yellow flowerpaste (gum paste) and roll it into a sausage shape, then flatten one half on your index finger using a palette knife. Paint over the full length with egg white, then place a hooked wire in the crease with the hook pointing away from the crease, fold over the paste and press together. Place on a lightly greased board and roll out the paste from the edge, so that a fatter part is left by the wire. Trim off the surplus with a craft knife. Also cut the other side so that it is in line with the wire. Lift off the board and bend the pointed end back a little for the centre of the flowers. Bend these forward and they could now be used as buds or centres.

2 Roll some more yellow paste a little thicker than usual and cut out the number of shapes required for the flowers using the No. 3 cutter. Keeping the remainder well covered, place one shape near the edge of a lightly greased board. Cut away the top half of both side (wing) petals and then shape them with the blunt end of a cocktail stick, on the edges only. Place on soft foam and curve the wing petals inwards towards the centre petal.

3 Using the blunt end of the cocktail stick, work the middle petal from the centre outwards, thereby spreading the paste. Then repeat on the other half. The complete petal should now look like the standard (back) petal of a sweet pea. Place the flower on soft

Flatten one half of the yellow paste sausage shape against your index finger.

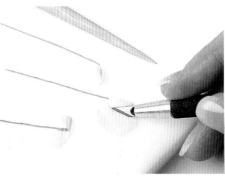

With the paste on the hooked wire, roll it out and cut away the surplus.

Thin the wing petals using the blunt end of a cocktail stick.

foam and indent the centre with a palette knife. Curve the petal edge on both sides with a leaf aid tool. Paint egg white onto the lowest part of the middle petal and position the bud (keel). Pick up the flower and pinch the back to make it more secure on the wire. Keep the keel in line with the wing petals.

LEAVES

4 (For full instructions on making and colouring leaves, see pages 62–5.) There are often three leaves at the base of each flower stalk, although the plant may look better balanced if the first flower on the stem has just one. The leaves should be pointed and very small, perhaps only about 1.5cm (⅝in) long and 2.5mm (⅛in) wide, with the middle one slightly longer than the other two. (In some varieties the leaves do not appear until quite late on, when the flowers are nearly over.) Make the leaves with 30-gauge green wires. When dry, paint with Fern droplet colour and gum arabic solution on the top side only.

END BUD

5 Form a bud (growing tip) for the end of the stem by cutting a piece of half-width florist's tape approximately 2cm (¾in) long. Twist half the length, bend this over and squash together, leaving the remaining half flat. This end can then be used to bind the bud onto the wire.

ASSEMBLY

6 Tape the flowers onto 24-gauge green wire using half-width florist's tape, with about 2.5cm (1in) in between them. The flowers should each have a little stem, about 5mm (¼in) long. Using half-width tape, join three leaves together, making sure that none of the stems are showing, and position these at the base of the flower stem. You can then position one broom flower plus leaf or leaves approximately 2.5cm (1in) from the next group, or further apart at about 5cm (2in), depending on the type of effect that you want to create. Dust a little Sunflower dusting powder onto the edges of the petals and buds to finish.

Curve the wing petals inwards towards the centre petal.

Thin down the middle petal, working from the centre outwards.

Indent the centre of the flower and then curve the edges with a leaf aid tool.

Carnation

YOU WILL NEED

Cutter No. 15

Flowerpaste (gum paste) coloured
  with Melon paste food colour
  (or colour of your choice) for
  flowers, Christmas Green for buds,
  Christmas Green plus a little Heraldic
  Black droplet colour to make grey-
  green for calyx and leaves

28- and 26-gauge green wires

30-gauge white wire

White florist's tape

Yellow dusting powder

Heraldic Black droplet colour

Hard foam

Soft foam

Small balling tool

Although you can form this flower in a calyx which has been made and dried in advance, it is quicker and easier to start at the centre, adding the calyx to the finished flower. This also allows you to stop after three worked shapes to form a flower that is just opening.

FLOWER

1 Tape together two 26-gauge green wires with white florist's tape and hook the end. Roll out some coloured flowerpaste (gum paste) and cut out several shapes using the No. 15 cutter. You will probably need six shapes to make one complete flower head. Keeping the others covered, place one shape on the edge of a lightly greased board. Make small, definite cuts along the edges of the three petals with a craft knife.

2 Start on the left-hand petal if you are right-handed. Using the blunt end of a cocktail stick, work each half of the petal for the full length. As each petal is thinned, fold it out of the way so that you have room to work the next. They should all double in size, particularly along the top edge.

3 Place the shape on hard foam, or on the hard part of the palm of your hand. Position the pointed end of the cocktail stick along the full length of the petal and rock until the sides of the paste curl upwards. Place the shape on soft foam and gently curve the ends of the petals with a small balling tool.

4 Cut a V shape from the base and then press the sides in towards the centre, until it is all one piece again. With the pointed end of the cocktail

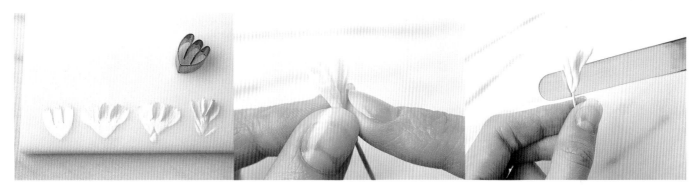

Shape the petals in several stages and shear away surplus paste from the base.

Wrap the petals around two hooked wires, taped together with white tape.

Use a palette knife to pick up and place the petals in position.

stick pressed into the petals, gather them together, and then shear away any surplus paste from the bottom part with a knife. Paint egg white on the base. Pick up the petals with a palette knife and wrap around the hooked wire.

5 Place the next two shapes on either side of the centre as they are worked, and then the last three or four around the whole flower. Avoid too much build-up of paste below the petals, removing the surplus with scissors or your fingers as it could become too bulky for the calyx.

CALYX

6 Form a cone from green flowerpaste about 2cm (³⁄₄in) long, that is pointed at one end and slightly rounded at the other. Hollow out the narrow end about halfway down. Thin down the rim using a cocktail stick and cut out five V shapes. At the stem end make two cuts, opposite each other, by sliding the blades of a pair of scissors over the paste until they are nearly together, and then making a little snip. Repeat in between but lower down. Push

the points back into the calyx, so that they are not sticking out. Paint egg white inside and slide into position below the petals.

BUDS

7 These are not essential, but are easy to make if required. Tape together two 28-gauge green wires with half-width white florist's tape and hook one end. Form a pointed cone from green flowerpaste and snip the rounded base in the same way as for the calyx of the open flower (see step 6). Dip the wire in egg white and pull through the bud – the end may need to be reshaped back to a point. Allow to dry, then dust the pointed tip with a little yellow dusting powder.

LEAVES

8 (For full instructions on making leaves, see pages 62–4.) Make the leaves with 30-gauge white wires. You may need to add white paste to the grey-green to achieve the shade you require. Cut out a number of narrow, pointed leaves of varying lengths and tape several of these around the base of each flower stem.

9 If you want to add the small curved leaves to the stem, bind quarter-width white florist's tape around the stem in one place to build up a thickened part. Roll out some grey-green paste very thinly on a lightly greased board and cut out one narrow shape, about 2.5cm (1in) long, which will give you two leaves. Lift the shape off the board carefully using a palette knife, place on soft foam and indent sharply with the palette knife through the centre. Paint the centre with egg white and very carefully slide the leaves up the wire to a point just above the thickened stem, then pinch them into place. Curve both sides gently with your fingers.

Slide the calyx up the wire and into position below the petals.

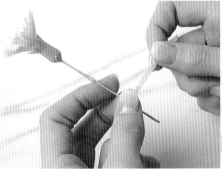

Bind white tape around the stem to build up a thick area for the small leaves.

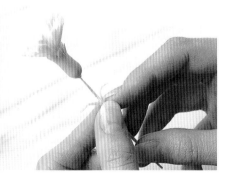

Attach the leaves just above the thickened part and pinch into place.

Chrysanthemum

Chrysanthemums are an essential part of the autumn palette and it is much easier to achieve good results with the method below than with the usual daisy cutter. Make a number of blooms, dust with appropriate colours when dry and then steam lightly to blend.

FLOWER

1 Cut two 8cm (3in) lengths of 24-gauge green wire for each flower and tape together with florist's tape. Hook one end, dip in egg white and cover with a small blob of green flowerpaste (gum paste). Snip the upper surface with scissors and allow to dry.

2 Using the Nos. 15 and 16 cutters, cut out five large shapes and five small from cream flowerpaste (to make one full flower). You can stop at almost any stage, provided the flower has a rounded shape overall.

3 Keeping the other shapes covered, place one of the small shapes on a lightly greased board. Cut each petal at least three times with a craft knife, thus producing several petals on each 'finger'. Roll each petal with the shoulder of a cocktail stick. If any of the petals have joined back together again, cut free with scissors. Place the petals on soft foam and curl them inwards using a leaf aid tool.

4 Dip the dried flower centre in egg white. Paint egg white on the base of the petal shape and at least halfway up, and wrap it around the centre. Bend the petals in towards the centre and remove any surplus underneath with your fingers.

5 Work the remaining small shapes in the same way, fixing them on

Snip the upper surface of the green flower centre with sharp scissors.

Cut the shape to produce several petals on each of the original 'fingers'.

Curl the petals inwards on soft foam using a leaf aid tool.

either side and placing the last two across the small gaps. After fixing each layer of petals, remove the surplus paste underneath.

6 Now work the large shapes. Prepare the next two following step 3, and fix these across the two previous joins. Again remove the surplus paste.

7 Cut the final three shapes twice to each 'finger', producing three petals. Thin down as before (see step 3), and cut with scissors if they have joined back together again. Turn over, place on soft foam and curl the petals backwards with a leaf aid tool, then fix around the flower. By this time the flower will be larger and you may need two shapes and an extra couple of 'fingers' (six petals), or even the three complete shapes. When dry, dust with your chosen colour.

CALYX
8 Using slightly thicker green flowerpaste, cut out the calyx using the No. 30 cutter. Thin down the edges with your fingers to make the calyx large enough to cover the slight

bulge at the back of the flower. Mark the back of the calyx with scissor cuts, starting from the centre and working out until you reach the edge. Turn the paste over, place it on the soft foam, and curve the shape with a dogbone tool. Paint the uncut side with egg white and slide into position behind the petals.

BUDS
9 Cut 5cm (2in) lengths of 28-gauge green wire, hook one end and dip in egg white. Take a small piece of green flowerpaste, form it into a ball and mark from the centre top down to the stem all the way round, using the back of a craft knife or the

hooked end of a leaf aid tool. Pull the wire through and pinch the paste into place. Allow to dry. Cover the wire with half-width florist's tape.

LEAVES
10 (For full instructions on making and colouring leaves, see pages 62–5.) Using green flowerpaste and the No. 31 cutter and/or real leaves, make some small leaves to go close to the flower head, and some larger ones for further down the stem. Use 28-gauge green wires for large leaves and 30-gauge for small ones. When dry, paint the leaves, buds and calyces with a mixture of Fern droplet colour and gum arabic solution.

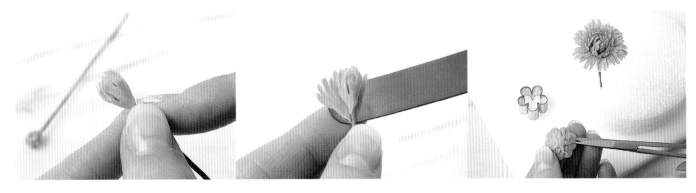

Wrap the petal shape around the flower centre and bend the petals inwards.

Place the newly wrapped petals in position using a palette knife.

Use scissors to mark the back of the calyx, working outwards to the edge.

Clematis

YOU WILL NEED

Cutter Nos 9, 23 and 24
   (25–28 optional)
Flowerpaste (gum paste) coloured with
   Royal Blue droplet colour and mixed
   with a little pink paste for flowers
   (or colour of your choice), Christmas
   Green paste food colour for leaves
28- and 24-gauge green wires
30-gauge white wire
Nile green florist's tape
Cream cotton thread
Yellow dusting powder or Burgundy
   droplet colour
Dusting powder in stronger shade
   than flower colour
Fern droplet colour
Gum arabic solution
Kitchen paper
Soft foam
Ripple foam with hole pushed through
   (position marked with a pen)

You can make this flower quite big and showy without losing the overall delicate feel of the plant. Perhaps use just one flower with several leaves on a stem as the only decoration on top of a cake. There is a good colour range in the four- to eight-petalled blooms.

STAMENS

1 Make the stamens following the instructions on page 10, winding the cream cotton thread around your fingers about 50 times and using two 5cm (2in) lengths of 30-gauge white wire. Tape the stamens plus twisted wires to 24-gauge green wires (two for each stem) with florist's tape. Dip the threads into egg white and leave them to dry and stiffen. When dry, pull down the threads and curl the lengths upwards, but leave a small cluster in the middle and cut these to just over 5mm (¼in) long.

2 Either paint egg white onto the ends of the stamens and then dip them in yellow dusting powder, or dilute a drop of Burgundy droplet colour with water, dip the stamen ends in this liquid and immediately blot with kitchen paper (to prevent the colour running too far down the threads). Use a paintbrush to touch the centre short stamens lightly with colour and blot immediately.

FLOWER

3 Form a ball of coloured flowerpaste (gum paste) the size of a large marble. Flatten and thin around the edges with your fingers. Place on a board and roll out, leaving a pimple of thicker paste in the middle. Cut out the shape on a dry part of the board using the No. 9 cutter, with the pimple still on the upper surface.

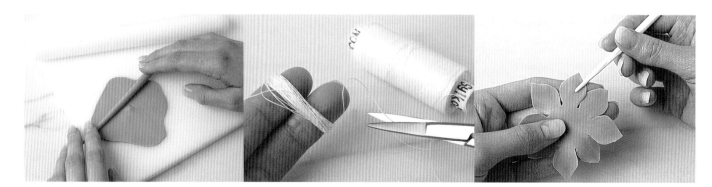

Roll out the paste for the flower, leaving a thicker 'pimple' in the centre.

To begin the stamens, wrap the thread around your fingers about 50 times.

For texture, work the edge of each petal in turn over your index finger.

4 Working on a lightly greased area of the board and using the sharp end of a cocktail stick, work both halves of each petal in turn. If you want a rounded end to the petal, roll over the point with the cocktail stick. As each petal is worked, lift it gently upwards so that there is room for the next petal to spread. Repeat all the way around the shape. If the paste hasn't dried too much, turn the shape over (pimple underneath) and work the edge of each petal over your index finger with the sharp end of the cocktail stick or other tool.

5 Lay the flower on soft foam and then indent through the centre of each petal using a leaf aid tool. Place the flower back on the board and lightly indent continuation lines from the base of the petals through to the centre.

6 Paint egg white on the wire behind the stamen threads and push this stem down through the flower and pimple (which is underneath) until the stamens are in position. Pinch from behind to secure. Push the stem through ripple foam using the pre-made hole until the petals just sit lightly and are supported: do not pull through too far. Allow to dry without moving the flower.

7 Holding the flower head carefully, dust the petals with a stronger colour, making sure your fingers support it well at the back throughout. Do not worry if the flower comes away from the stamens: mix a little of the same coloured flowerpaste with some egg white and paint this in and around the hole underneath, then settle the stamens in place again and allow to dry.

LEAVES

8 (For full instructions on making and colouring leaves, see pages 62–5.) Make the leaves using 28-gauge green wires. Using cutter Nos 23 and 24 (and smaller shapes if required), cut out a centre leaf and two side leaves, vein with the leaf aid tool, and give each one a slight bend. When dry, tape the leaves together with florist's tape and paint with Fern droplet colour and gum arabic solution. Make several groups of different-sized leaves.

Working on soft foam, indent along the centre of each petal using a leaf aid tool.

Push the stamen wire down through the centre of the flower and pull into place.

Tape the leaves together in groups of three using florist's tape.

Cornflower

YOU WILL NEED

Cutter No. 15

Flowerpaste (gum paste) coloured with
Royal Blue and French Pink droplet
colours (to make mauve-violet) for
flower centre, Royal Blue for petals,
Christmas Green paste food colour
for calyx and leaves

30- and 26-gauge nile green wires

Nile green florist's tape

African Violet and/or Ultramarine
dusting powders

Black pencil

Thick black stamen thread

Hard foam

Soft foam

Generally thought of as blue, annual cornflowers actually come in a range of colours. Each flower is made up of many florets, but these are time consuming to make, so this method creates an impression of the flower rather than an accurate copy.

FLOWER CENTRE

1 Form a cone from mauve-violet flowerpaste (gum paste) about 5mm (¼in) long and slightly less across the open end. Tape together two 8cm (3in) lengths of 26-gauge green wire with florist's tape. Hook the wire, dip in egg white and pull through the cone. Using sharp, pointed scissors, cut the top surface all over, especially all around the edge. Push in about five 5mm (¼in) lengths of thick black stamen thread. Allow to dry, preferably overnight.

FLOWER

2 Roll out some blue flowerpaste and cut out about eight pieces using the No. 15 cutter. The exact number depends on the size of the cone and how well you bunch the petals. Work on one shape at a time, starting with the left-hand petal if you are right-handed. Place the shape on the edge of a lightly greased board. Using a cocktail stick, spread the paste out from the centre one way and then the other to form a triangular shape (you may need to change the direction of the cocktail stick). The paste should now be stuck to the board; cut out four or five deep V shapes along the edge of this petal using a craft knife.

3 For extra shaping, place the shoulder of the cocktail stick on the points, one at a time, and rock it

Work the petals in stages with a cocktail stick to achieve the required shape.

Gather the petals together and remove any surplus paste using a craft knife.

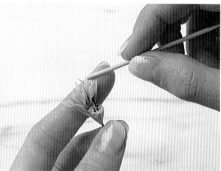

Bend the outer petals over your index finger, using a cocktail stick.

from side to side. This will change the shape from a point to a curve. Fold the shape over, work the middle petal in the same way, and then the last one. Place the shape on hard foam, or the hard part of the palm of your hand, position the shoulder of the cocktail stick at the base of the first petal, tipping it downwards very slightly, and rock. This action should bring the sides up, forming a floret. Repeat this action on the other two petals.

4 Cut out a V shape from the base and then, working on a lightly greased board, press the sides towards the centre, until it is all one piece again. With the pointed end of the cocktail stick pressed into the petals, gather them together, squash the paste at the base, and then shear away any surplus from the bottom part of the shape with a craft knife.

5 Paint egg white onto the paste below the petals, pick up on a palette knife and place in position on the side of the dried cone. Curve back the tiny outer petals over your index finger using a cocktail stick.

6 Continue working each shape in the same way. As you add petals, overlap the previous one slightly, until the flower is complete.

CALYX

7 Form a fairly rounded cone shape 2cm (¾in) long from green flowerpaste. Using the pointed end of a cocktail stick, hollow out the narrow end, then cut out five rough V shapes around the rim. Cut V shapes on the calyx using scissors, then paint egg white into the cavity of the calyx and pull the flower through into position.

8 Allow to dry, then dust the flower with African Violet and/or Ultramarine dusting powder. Use a black pencil to mark in the fringed effect on the surface of the calyx.

LEAVES

9 (For full instructions on making leaves, see pages 62–4.) Cornflower leaves are usually short, narrow and pointed. Make them on 5cm (2in) lengths of 30-gauge green wire. Cut out the required shape, about 5mm (¼in) wide and 2.5–4cm (1–1½in) long. Lift the shape off the board carefully with a palette knife, place it on soft foam and then indent the main vein with the side of the palette knife. Curve the leaf slightly and then put it on one side to dry. Make about three leaves for each flower stem.

BUDS

10 Make a small pointed cone from green flowerpaste and mark in the same way as for the calyx on the full open flower (see step 8).

Attach each petal piece in turn, overlapping them slightly as you go.

Cut V shapes on the calyx with scissors before the flower is pulled into place.

When the calyx is in position, mark a fringed effect with a black pencil.

Cyclamen

YOU WILL NEED

Cutter Nos 14 and 34

Flowerpaste (gum paste) coloured with
French Pink droplet colour (or left
white) for flowers, pale Christmas
Green paste food colour for calyx
and leaves

28- and 24-gauge green wires

Beige florist's tape

French Pink and Holly Leaf
droplet colours

White stamen thread

Gum arabic solution

Cotton wool bud

Cyclamen flowers range from pure white, through various shades of pink, to deep magenta. The plant looks very delicate, yet is quite easy to make. To give it more character, make up lots of leaves in different sizes and shades of green.

PETALS, CALYX AND PISTIL

1 Tape together two 16cm (6½in) 24-gauge green wires with half-width florist's tape and hook one end. Form a small cone from pink flowerpaste and hollow out until about 5mm (¼in) across. Dip the wire in egg white and pull through. When dry, bend the wire into an S.

2 Cut out a calyx from green flowerpaste using the No. 34 cutter. Paint the rounded end of the cone with egg white and fix the calyx firmly in place. (Alternatively, this can be done before the wire is bent.)

3 Using the No. 14 cutter, cut out two petal shapes from pink (or white) flowerpaste. Place one near the edge of a lightly greased board and cut the petals to a pointed shape, then work on one petal using the shoulder of a cocktail stick, until the required shape is achieved. When you have shaped all three petals, cut off the point at their base.

4 Lightly indent the paste below the petals by pressing down the point of the cocktail stick – do not cut the paste. This gives the impression that all the petals are separate. Pick up the petals and twist each one in turn.

5 Holding the shape with the flat end balanced over the end of your thumb, paint the base with egg white

Work the petals in stages to achieve the finished shape.

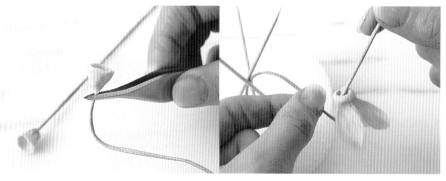

Bend the wire holding the central cone into an S shape for ease of working.

Fix on the first petal shape, pushing the paste inside the dried central cone.

for about 1cm (½in). Fix onto the cone opposite the wire and push a little of the shape inside using a blunt cocktail stick. Ensure the petals are stuck both inside and out.

6 Cut one petal off the second shape and work the other two as before, then again cut off the bottom point. Fix in place so that a petal lies on either side of the wire. Allow to dry.

7 To make the pistil, paint egg white into the cone, push in a tiny piece of pink (or white) flowerpaste and then put a short length of white stamen thread in the centre, so that it just shows above the rim. Allow to dry.

8 Turn the flower over and straighten the stem. Paint a deeper colour at the petal base (pink on white flowers), then brush upwards gently with a clean, damp paintbrush to remove any hard edges. Paint the same colour on the stalk and rub it up and down with your fingers.

BUDS

9 Form a pointed cone from pink (or white) flowerpaste about 1cm (½in)

across. Cut two 5cm (2in) lengths of 28-gauge green wire, tape together with half-width beige tape and hook one end. Dip in egg white and pull through the cone. Mark the length of the paste five times with a palette knife, roll between your fingers and twist the shape from the point. Cut out a calyx from green flowerpaste, paint with egg white and fix on the rounded end of the cone.

LEAVES

10 (For full instructions on making and colouring leaves, see pages 62–5.) Cut two 8cm (3in) 28-gauge green wires and tape together with beige tape. Cut out a number of heart-shaped leaves freehand (see page 126) from pale green flowerpaste, in different sizes. Using a serrator, cut away at the edge, leaving a nice rounded shape. Lift the leaf carefully off the board and place a leaf aid tool firmly on the wire at the leaf base.

Bend the wire until the stalk is nearly at right angles to the paste. Hold the stalk between two fingers and indent the main veins on the upper surface, with your palm supporting the leaf. Allow to dry.

11 Paint the top of the leaf with Holly Leaf droplet colour and gum arabic solution, then remove with a cocktail stick to make the veins. Use a cotton wool bud to remove paint to make the light patches near the edge.

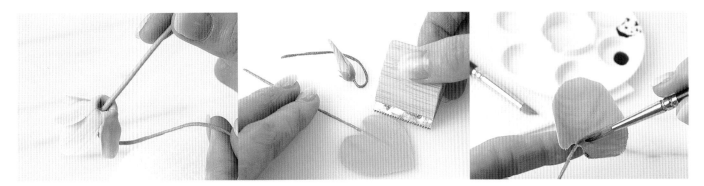

Fix on the second shape so that the petals lie on either side of the wire.

Use a serrator to work on the edge of the heart-shaped leaf.

Paint the leaf with Holly Leaf droplet colour and gum arabic solution.

Daffodil

As there is such a range of sizes in this flower, from tiny jonquils to narcissi and the larger daffodils, you can choose a size to fit the size and design of your cake. The method of making the blooms is a lot easier than the usual one, and the finished flowers more realistic.

YOU WILL NEED

Cutter No. 18 (or smaller sizes, Nos 19–21)

Flowerpaste (gum paste) coloured with Melon paste food colour for flowers, Christmas Green for leaves, Bamboo droplet colour for husk

28- and 26-gauge green wires

Nile green florist's tape

Fern droplet colour

Cream, deep yellow (such as Tangerine or Saffron), Oak, Pistachio and Eucalyptus dusting powders

Gum arabic solution

Yellow stamen thread

Corn-on-the-cob husk (optional)

Soft foam

FLOWER

1 Cut two appropriate lengths of 26-gauge green wire and hook the end of one (unless you are making very small flowers, in which case leave the wire straight).

2 To make the trumpet, form a small cone from yellow flowerpaste (gum paste), about 3cm (1¼in) long and 5mm (¼in) across at the wide end. Using the blunt end of a cocktail stick, hollow out the wide end to the depth of the trumpet, thinning down the paste against your index finger. Cut out three shallow V shapes around the rim with sharp scissors.

3 Working on a board, frill the edge of the trumpet with the blunt end of the cocktail stick. If you want a turned-back edge, hold the cone at right angles to the edge of the board and frill again. Plenty of cornflour (cornstarch) on the cocktail stick and board will make this process easier. To form the ridges on the outside of the trumpet, roll it against corn-on-the-cob husk or use a cocktail stick; on the inside, simply press the pointed end of the cocktail stick into the paste all the way round.

4 Dip the hooked wire in egg white and pull through the cone. To make the paste really fine on the wire below the trumpet, 'squash' the paste and then trim off the excess on both sides of the wire. Cut three 5mm (¼in) lengths of yellow stamen thread and push into the trumpet. There should really be a total of six stamens and a pistil, but with these smaller flowers there is not enough room. Allow the cone to dry, preferably overnight.

Cut and reshape the petals in stages to achieve the finished result.

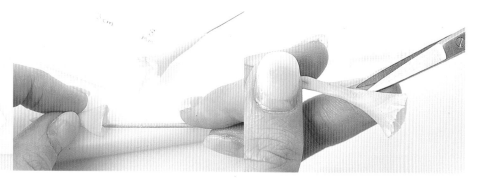

Hollow out the cone for the trumpet with the blunt end of a cocktail stick.

Trim off excess paste from the sides of the trumpet using sharp scissors.

5 Roll out some yellow flowerpaste and cut out the six-petal shape using the No. 18 cutter, making sure the paste is not too thin. Cut three alternate petals to one shape and then the others to a different shape as shown. Work the petals with a cocktail stick, making sure that the first three alternate petals are wide at the base, then work the remaining petals. The first three should come forward automatically. Give shape to the petals by working them on soft foam, bending three back and then curving three forward, using a leaf aid tool. Work on the edges of three petals to curve them slightly, and put some ridges down the centre of each shape with a leaf aid tool. Mark a continuation line from the base of the petals right to the centre with the hooked end of the leaf aid tool.

6 Paint the base of the centre (below the trumpet) with egg white and then slide the six-petal shape into position. Pinch the paste at the back to secure.

7 Tape on the second length of wire with florist's tape, for the full length

of the first wire that shows below the flower throat. Form a small oval shape from green flowerpaste and slightly dent one end, using the blunt end of a cocktail stick. Paint the top of the green shape with egg white and slide it into place directly below the throat of the flower, hiding where the second wire joins. Bend over the completed flower head just a little. Paint the middle of the backs of the petals and the throat with diluted Fern droplet colour.

HUSK

8 Roll out some beige flowerpaste extremely thinly. Cut out a rough oval shape, bearing in mind the size of your daffodil. Thin down again using a cocktail stick: starting from the centre, roll with a rocking action and a lot of pressure, which will texture the husk. This should be very fine and crumpled-looking, so you can actually tear it slightly at the edges to make it look more realistic. Turn the paste over and place on soft foam. Indent through the middle with a palette knife, then curl the edges using a leaf aid tool – if the paste is sticky, dip the tool in

cornflour first. Paint the base of the husk with egg white and position on the stalk just below the flower. If you find this difficult with your fingers, leave the husk on the soft foam and press the stalk onto it. Crumple the husk before the paste hardens.

COLOURING

9 Dust the flowers with deeper yellow, such as Tangerine or Saffron, on the trumpet and petal edges. Dust the husk with Oak and Pistachio.

LEAVES

10 Follow the instructions on page 67. Tape two or three leaves to the base of each flower stem.

Pinch the paste at the back to secure the petals in place on the trumpet.

Thin down and texture the husk with a cocktail stick, using a rocking action.

Using egg white, secure the husk just below the flower.

Daisy

Sometimes a flower becomes too familiar, and we no longer notice the details that make up its unique character. A rosette of leaves, together with a bud low down in the centre, help to make a beautiful arrangement from something we dig out of our lawns!

FLOWERS AND BUD

1 Cut and hook a 5cm (2in) length of 24-gauge green wire. Form a little ball of green flowerpaste (gum paste), making sure it is the same size as the centre of the daisy cutter. Dip the hooked end of the wire into egg white, pull it through the paste and flatten into a dome shape. Allow to dry. Paint the top part of the shape only with egg white and then dip it into Forsythia dusting powder.

2 Form a little ball of green flowerpaste for the bud, dip a hooked 24-gauge green wire in egg white and pull through the ball. Indent the paste heavily from the centre top down to the stem, using a leaf aid tool.

3 Roll out some white flowerpaste and cut out one or two petal shapes per flower using the No. 36 cutter. Working on a lightly greased board, cut each petal in half (or into three, if you feel confident enough!). Roll each petal with the blunt end of a cocktail stick. Place the petals on soft foam and curve them using a leaf aid tool, then work with a circular movement in the middle of the shape with a dogbone tool. Paint the centre of the shape with egg white and push into place around the prepared flower centre.

CALYX

4 For this flower you will need to make sure you keep the calyx small, neat and tidy. Roll out some slightly thicker green flowerpaste and cut out the calyx shape using a No. 30 cutter, then cut out some small V shapes around the edge. Thin down the edges with your fingers to make the

Make the flower centre from green flowerpaste and dip in Forsythia powder.

Cut out the petal shape and then cut each petal in half or into three.

Thin the petals by rolling each one with the blunt end of a cocktail stick.

calyx large enough to cover the slight bulge at the back of the flower. Mark the back of the calyx with a series of scissor cuts, starting from the centre and working outwards until you reach the edge. Turn the paste over, place it on the soft foam and work the shape with a dogbone tool in order to curve it. Paint the uncut side of the shape with egg white and slide the calyx carefully into position just behind the petals of the flower.

COLOURING

5 Allow the flower to dry thoroughly, then dust a little Garnette dusting powder onto the backs of the petals, provided that this shading fits in with your overall colour scheme – not all daisies feature this touch of red colour.

LEAVES

6 (For full instructions on making and colouring leaves, see pages 62–5.) Make the leaves with 28-gauge green wires. Using pale green flowerpaste, make a number of leaves, cutting out the required shapes freehand – some small and some large (see page 126).

Make some little nicks along the edges with a craft knife. Indent through the middle of the leaf with a leaf aid tool, and curve the whole shape a little. Allow to dry, then paint with Holly Leaf droplet colour and gum arabic solution, leaving a wide vein unpainted in the centre of the leaf.

ASSEMBLY

7 Tape the wires for the flowers and bud with nile green florist's tape. There is no need to tape the leaf wires as they will not actually be visible in the final arrangement. Assemble with the flowers and bud in the centre, surrounded by a circle of leaves of different sizes that are taped together.

On soft foam, curl the petals up by working the centre with a dogbone tool.

Make the bud from green paste and indent it heavily from top to bottom.

Paint the leaves, leaving a wide vein unpainted in the middle.

Dianthus

YOU WILL NEED

Cutter No. 6

Flowerpaste (gum paste) coloured with French Pink droplet colour (or left white) for flowers, pale Christmas Green paste food colour for calyx, Christmas Green plus a little Heraldic Black droplet colour to make grey-green for leaves

26-gauge green wire

30-gauge white wire

White florist's tape

White stamen thread

Small balling tool (optional)

Soft foam

There is a huge number of varieties within the *Dianthus* – or pink – family and I have chosen here to make the little single-flowered type rather than the many-petalled, larger carnation. The foliage of these pretty flowers has quite a distinctive grey-green colouring, although this differs between varieties.

FLOWER

1 Form some pink or white flowerpaste (gum paste) into a marble-sized ball, flatten all around the edges with your fingers and then pull up a slender cone in the middle. Roll out the paste all around this central column and then cut out the petal shape with the No. 6 cutter. Using a craft knife, cut away the paste in between the individual petals, to make them separate right up to the throat.

2 Cut into the outer edge with little cuts, so that as you thin and spread each petal by working it with a cocktail stick you will have a fringed edge. Lightly curve the ends of these petals on soft foam using a small balling tool or leaf aid tool. Open up the small throat of the flower with the pointed end of the cocktail stick. Cut an 8cm (3in) length of 26-gauge green wire and tape with half-width white florist's tape. Hook the end of the wire, dip it in egg white and pull it through the flower throat. Check that the throat remains slender, and if necessary cut away any surplus paste with scissors. If the throat is particularly slender there may not be enough room for a hook, so if this is the case leave the wire straight.

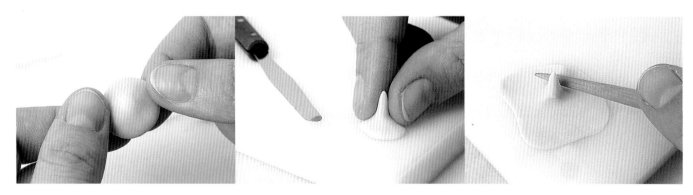

Flatten all around the edges of the ball of paste using your fingers.

Pull up a slender cone of paste from the middle of the flattened ball.

Roll out the paste all around the central column, ready for cutting out the shape.

3 Cut two 1cm (½in) lengths of white stamen thread. Curve one end of each length and bend at right angles using tweezers, then insert in the throat.

CALYX

4 Like the throat of the flower, the calyx is very slender and quite long. Form a cone about 1cm (½in) long from pale green paste and roll it between your fingers until it is pointed at one end. Using the pointed end of a cocktail stick, open up the narrow end and hollow out about half the length. Cut out at least five V shapes around the rim using scissors and thin down the edges with the cocktail stick. Using scissors, make two V-shaped cuts at the base of the calyx opposite each other, and then cut again slightly higher up to form four V shapes in all. Push these back in flush with the surface of the calyx. Paint egg white inside, then slide the calyx into position behind the flower head and pinch into place, leaving a gap of about 5mm (¼in) – the flower usually grows slightly away from the calyx as it matures.

LEAVES

5 (For full instructions on making leaves, see pages 62–4.) Using 30-gauge white wires, make the leaves from grey-green flowerpaste, cutting the shapes freehand (see page 126). Vary the length, keeping them narrow and pointed, with a good indentation through the centre of each one. (A palette knife works best for cutting and indenting these leaves.) When dry, tape all the leaves together with white florist's tape, positioning them at the base around the smallest leaf and using progressively bigger leaves as you join in the rest around the flower stem at roughly the same point.

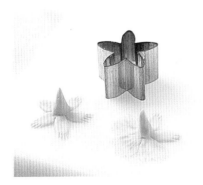

Cut out the petal shape around the central column.

Lightly curve the ends of the fringed petals with a balling or leaf aid tool.

Slide the calyx into place behind the flower head and pinch to secure.

Eustoma

This flower is a great favourite with florists due to its delicate pink, purple, apricot or cream colouring and the fact that it is fairly long lasting when cut. The buds are such a pretty shape that it is well worth buying a spray of flowers in order to study the real thing.

YOU WILL NEED

Cutter Nos 13 and 14

Flowerpaste (gum paste) left white for bud calyx, coloured with African Violet dusting powder, French Pink droplet colour or Melon paste food colour for flowers, cream for large buds, pale Christmas Green for tiny buds, Christmas Green plus a little Heraldic Black droplet colour to make grey-green for flower calyx and leaves

30-, 28- and 24-gauge green wires

30-gauge white wire

Yellow, nile green and olive florist's tape

Cream and Dark Eucalyptus dusting powders, plus shade to match flower colour

Paint Aid

FLOWER

1 To make the stamens, bind yellow florist's tape around 30-gauge white wire at short intervals, then cut halfway along a length of the tape and halfway along the adjoining the wire. You will need five stamens per flower. To form the pistil, cover 30-gauge white wire with half-width nile green florist's tape and bend into the shape shown on page 124.

2 Cover two 24-gauge green wires with olive florist's tape and hook one end. Decide on the colour of the flower and use this flowerpaste (gum paste) to make a cup shape about 1cm (½in) long and 5mm (¼in) across at the open end with a slender, narrow base. Dip the hooked wire in egg white and pull through. Push in five stamens and place the pistil in the centre. Allow to dry overnight.

3 Cut out two petal shapes using the No. 13 cutter and cut off one petal (making five). Lay the three-petal shape on the edge of a lightly greased board and cut the petals to a point from about halfway down. Begin working on the left-hand petal (if you are right-handed). Using the pointed end of a cocktail stick, work from the middle of the petal outwards in a fan shape. The action is press, rock twice on the same place, then lift the cocktail stick and re-position. When the petal is the required shape, fold it over and work the middle one, followed by the one on the right. Turn the petals back, and they will overlap. Turn one side edge of each petal over the cocktail stick to curl. Thin down the paste on the bottom V shape slightly to make it large enough to fit around the cup. Paint this shape with egg white and stick

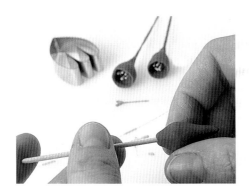

Make sure there is a slender base to the cone.

Shape the petals one by one, working left to right (if you are right-handed).

Stick the three-petal shape around the central cup using egg white.

the petals to the dried cup. Hang upside down while you work the two-petal shape in the same way.

4 Thin down and paint the base of these petals with egg white as before and stick onto the cup shape in the remaining space, tucking one side in under the previous shape. Allow to dry hanging upside down. Paint just the narrow base of the petals with Paint Aid and cream dusting powder.

CALYX
5 Roll out some grey-green flowerpaste very thinly and cut out five strips about 2.5cm (1in) long and 2.5mm (⅛in) wide. Put one over your index finger, paint with egg white and then press onto the flower from the base up, between the petals, leaving the last bit unattached.

BUDS
6 For the larger buds, make a cone of cream flowerpaste, again with a slender base and about 2.5cm (1in) long, and indent from the wide end above the narrow part to the tip with a fine palette knife. Hook a 28-gauge green wire, dip in egg white and

then pull through the cone. Twist the cone from the pointed end. Make and fix on a calyx as for the open flower (see step 5). Dust down about half the bud from the pointed end with a powder colour to match the open flower.

7 Make tiny buds from pale green flowerpaste using 30-gauge green wires. Pick up the paste for most of the length of the cone with straight tweezers to give the effect of a calyx. Using Dark Eucalyptus powder and water or Paint Aid, match up the green and paint these raised ridges.

8 For a bud about to open, make a cone about 1cm (½in) long, with a narrow piece under the base. Allow to dry. Cut out five petals as for the flower (see step 3) using the No. 14 cutter. Cut the petals to points, reshape and then position around the dried centre. Dust colour at the top of the petals. Make and fix on a calyx as for the open flower (see step 5).

LEAVES
9 (For full instructions on making leaves, see pages 62–4.) Make these leaves with 28-gauge green wires. Cut out a number of leaves freehand (see page 126) from grey-green flowerpaste, in varying sizes.

ASSEMBLY
10 Cover the flower and bud stems with olive florist's tape. Tape on the smallest bud about 5cm (2in) down the flower stem, with the bud stem roughly 3cm (1¼in) long. Use the smallest leaves at this point – there should be two leaves at each junction, but there is no need to be too precise with this. Bring in the other buds and leaves at intervals of about 4cm (1½in), varying the lengths of the stems.

Press the calyx strips onto the flower from the base upwards.

Pick up ridges of paste to give the impression of a calyx on the tiny buds.

The flowers are made in stages, then buds and leaves are added to complete.

Freesia

Unless they are to be white, you can make these flowers with off-white paste – add a tiny amount of yellow – as this takes powder colour much better. Many shades of this flower fade away to yellow at the base, while the stamen anthers tend to be the same colour as the flower.

You will need
Cutter No. 14

White or off-white flowerpaste (gum paste) for flowers (but coloured with Melon paste food colour for yellow), Christmas Green for buds and covers

28-, 26- and 24-gauge green wires

Scientific wire

White and olive florist's tape

Iris or Forsythia dusting powder

Fern droplet colour

Gum arabic solution

Kitchen paper

Make-up sponge

Soft foam

Ripple foam

Dusting powders for flowers
Baby Maize for base of all flowers and buds except white

Forsythia, Blood Orange and/or Garnette for yellow flowers

Mauve Mist or Iris for mauve flowers

African Violet brushed with Mauve Mist, or Empress Purple with Mauve Mist or Iris, for deep mauve flowers

Stamens

1 Colour a length of white florist's tape with Iris or Forsythia dusting powder (depending on the flower colour) following the instructions on page 7. Cut a length of scientific wire, pull to straighten, then roll the coloured tape around it at intervals with the length of two stamens (about 5cm/2in) between each roll of tape. Cut halfway along a length of wire, and halfway along the adjoining length of tape.

2 Tape three stamens securely onto a 10cm (4in) length of 24-gauge green wire with half-width white tape, using enough to build up a sausage shape. The stamens should not show above the petals in the finished flower. Take the tape a little way down the wire, then cover from the base of the 'sausage' to the bottom with olive tape.

Flowers

3 Cut out two petal shapes for each flower from white, off-white or yellow flowerpaste (gum paste) using the No. 14 cutter. Working on one shape on the edge of a lightly greased board, cut each petal to a point and then work the paste back out to the shape required, using the pointed end of a cocktail stick. Lift onto soft foam and curve the end as well as along the length.

4 Paint the bottom triangle with egg white, place the stamens in the middle, fold over one side, and then lift up and away from the foam and bring the other petal into place. Keeping the flower head facing down, press and shape the paste around the tape with your fingers. Allow to dry hanging upside down.

Cut the stamens halfway along a length of tape, then halfway along the wire.

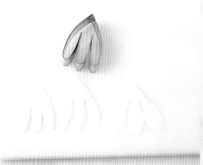

Cut the petals to a point and then work to the shape required.

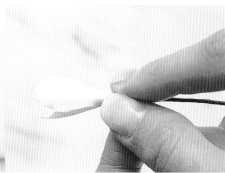

Press and shape the base of the flower around the tape with your fingers.

5 Take the second shape and cut to separate each petal. Work the first petal as before, keeping the others covered. When shaped, bend slightly and lay the petal on ripple foam. Work the other two petals in the same way.

6 Holding the first petal in your hand, paint egg white on the lower part and position over a gap on the first layer. Fix on the other two petals in the same way, splaying them out if you want a more open flower. Allow to dry before dusting with your chosen colour.

BUDS

7 Cover a 15cm (6in) length of 28-gauge green wire with half-width olive tape. Bend one end over, then hold the wire firmly at the base as you twist from the top with tweezers. Continue down the stem, bending out, back and twisting for every bud.

8 Paint each twist with egg white as you make the buds, and push on a small amount of green flowerpaste. Squash the stalk end, then with fine scissors cut away the surplus to make a small, neat bud. Cut V shapes on either side to form a bud cover.

Make an extra, larger bud on 28-gauge wire, indent the top three times and cut to make the bud cover.

9 For the bud about to open, cut and hook a short length of 26-gauge green wire. Shape some off-white flowerpaste to the size of a petal, dip the wire in egg white and pull through. When dry, cover with one petal, cut and worked as before (see steps 3 and 5). Paint egg white inside the petal and place on the dried shape so that one edge shows on the back of the curve. Do not move it around, as the dusting powder will not stick where you have painted egg white.

10 To make the bud cover, form a cone from green flowerpaste about 1.5cm ($^5/_8$in) long and 5mm ($^1/_4$in) across. Hollow it out and thin down using a cocktail stick, then cut two V shapes opposite each other. Paint in some egg white and position at the base of the bud. Make another and fix to the base of the flower.

COLOURING AND ASSEMBLY

11 Dust the flower with your chosen colour. Tape larger buds onto the group of smaller ones, then dust the smaller buds with baby maize powder and the larger buds with the same colour as the flower. Tape the flower to the spray of buds, bending the buds at a right angle to ensure you keep the flower and its wire straight. Shape the spray in a curve that will fit into your overall arrangement, remembering that the buds tend to lie in a herringbone pattern. Paint all the bud covers with a mixture of Fern droplet colour and gum arabic solution.

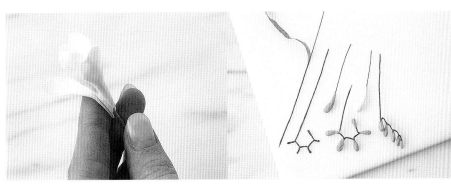

Fix on the petals so that they alternate with those in the previous layer.

Bend and twist the wire, then add small amounts of paste for the buds.

Make the bud cover from green paste and cut V shapes opposite each other.

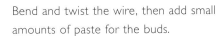

Gerbera

This is a very dramatic flower that comes in strong colours ranging from creams, yellows and oranges to deep cerise. When fresh, the petals tend to stand up in a fairly rigid manner – use just one shape for the main petals or add a smaller shape on an inner layer.

YOU WILL NEED

Cutter Nos 14 and 36

Flowerpaste (gum paste) coloured with French Pink droplet colour or Melon paste food colour for flowers, Christmas Green for calyx, flower centre and leaves

26- and 24-gauge green wires

Pipe cleaners

Nile green florist's tape

Dusting powder in colour of your choice for flowers (see step 5)

Yellow dusting powder for centre of pink or red flowers

Burgundy droplet colour for centre of cream, yellow or peach flowers

Fern droplet colour

Gum arabic solution

Aluminium foil

Blu-tack

Soft foam

CALYX

1 Tape together two 11.5cm (4½in) lengths of 24-gauge green wire with florist's tape and hook one end. Form a fat cone about 2cm (¾in) long from green flowerpaste (gum paste). Open up the narrow end and hollow it out using a cocktail stick, leaving enough thickness at the base to take the hooked wires comfortably. Thin down the rim of the cone until it is very fine and then cut out small V shapes all the way round. Place the points of a pair of straight, fine tweezers on either side of the cuts and squeeze the paste gently, then repeat this process in between these down to the base. Do not make the marks too regular or deep. Dip the wires in egg white and pull through the calyx. Tape on a pipe cleaner to thicken the stem. Allow to dry overnight.

2 Cut out two 10cm (4in) diameter circles of foil and form into a funnel shape by pleating all round. Make a hole in the middle and slide the funnel up the stem, to fit snugly beneath the calyx. Secure with Blu-tack directly underneath. Make sure the foil is right up against the calyx and slightly above the rim level.

FLOWER

3 Cut out six shapes from your chosen colour of flowerpaste using the No. 14 cutter. You can vary the size of each layer of petals, but this may slow you down.

4 Place one shape on the edge of a lightly greased board. Cut each petal in half for the full length using a palette knife and thin down by laying a pointed cocktail stick along the full length and gently pressing on just the

When the calyx is complete and dry, cut two circles of foil and pleat into a funnel.

Cut and work the petals in stages, until the required shape is achieved.

Curl the backs of the petals and fix them onto the flower in layers.

edges. The inner cut edges of each petal will need extra pressure to ensure the right shape is achieved, as they are slightly wider halfway along their length. There is no need to thin down the full width of the petals.

5 Turn the petals over and place on soft foam, then gently curl with a leaf aid tool. Turn the paste back to the right side, cut off a small triangle from the base and then cut out three V shapes along this edge. On a lightly greased part of the board, press the base together, which will curve the outer edge of the petals into an arc. Brush the petal backs or inside the calyx with egg white and fix the petals in place. This will be about one-third of the first layer. Complete the layer and then dust with a deeper colour.

6 Complete two layers of petals in this way, alternating the shapes, and dust powder colour on each layer as you go along.

FLOWER CENTRE
7 Cut out two shapes from coloured flowerpaste using the No. 36 cutter.

If the centre of the flower has a fairly large hole, fill in some paste so that the shapes do not sink too low. Working on one shape at a time, halve each petal and thin down with the blunt end of a cocktail stick. Place the shape on the soft foam and curve the petals inwards by moving a dogbone tool around quickly in the centre. Work the second shape in the same way. Paint egg white into the centre of first shape and place the second shape on top. Paint egg white into the middle of the flower and then place the two centre shapes neatly in position.

8 Form a cone from green flower-paste, about 5mm (¼in) long and slightly smaller in diameter than the opening in the centre of the flower. Cut many times across the flat end of the cone with fine-pointed scissors, especially around the edge. If you can, thin down the cuts on the edge with the blunt end of the cocktail stick. If there is very little depth in the middle of the flower centre, cut off most of the back of the cone with scissors. Check once more that the cone is not too big for the opening

in the middle of the flower, then paint in some egg white and insert the centre. Paint or dust according to the colour of the flower.

9 When the flower is dry, carefully remove the Blu-tack and then the foil. Paint the calyx with a mixture of Fern droplet colour and gum arabic solution.

LEAVES
10 Follow the instructions on page 67. When the leaves are complete, tape them on at the base of the flower stem, if required.

Place the two worked centre shapes one on top of the other and insert.

Make cuts in the central cone, then thin down the edge cuts with a cocktail stick.

Once the flower is assembled, paint or dust the centre with a suitable colour.

Iris

YOU WILL NEED

Cutter No. 7

Flowerpaste (gum paste) coloured with
    paste food colour of your choice for
    flowers, Christmas Green for leaves,
    Bamboo droplet colour for dead
    leaves, pale Bamboo for lower buds

30-, 26- and 24-gauge green wires

30-gauge white wire

Nile green florist's tape

Eucalyptus (or Eau-de-nil), Baby Maize,
    Iris, Pistachio, Oak and Forsythia
    dusting powders

Paint Aid

Corn-on-the-cob husk (optional)

Soft foam

Small balling tool

It is perfectly acceptable to scale down the larger iris varieties to make them practical for cake decorating. The delightful shape of the group of leaves is just as important as that of the flowers, and it is also essential to bring in the variations in colour for both.

FLOWER

1 Tape together two 10–13cm (4–5in) lengths of 26-gauge green wire with half-width florist's tape. Form a small cone from coloured flowerpaste (gum paste) that will be about 5mm (¼in) long and less across when hollowed out. Hook the wire, dip in egg white and pull through the cone. Allow to dry.

2 Cut out the shape for the 'fall' petals (which hang down) and, leaving the shape in the cutter, cut another to make thicker paste. Work the petals on a lightly greased board with a blunt cocktail stick, until each is well rounded, then rock the shoulder of the cocktail stick on the edge of the petals at intervals to get 'movement'. Turn the shape over on soft foam, paint egg white onto the rim of the little cone and press it

down onto the centre of the petals. Lift up the wire and petals, and press the petal shape into the cone with a small balling tool. Pull the petals right down.

3 Cut out two more petal shapes for each flower. On the first shape, cut the petals to the same length as their width. Cut a V shape from the end of each. Thin the edges only with a blunt cocktail stick. Place on soft foam and use a leaf aid tool to curl the paste by pulling it from the points to the centre. Paint the centre of the fall petals with egg white and place the little petals on top.

4 On the second shape, cut each petal to a point. On a lightly greased board, work the petals to the shape you want with a pointed cocktail stick. These are the 'standards'. Place

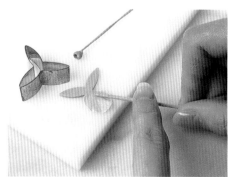

Work the edges of the 'fall' petals with a cocktail stick to achieve 'movement'.

Curl the little petals on soft foam using a leaf aid tool.

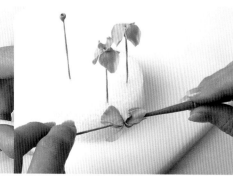

Lift the finished 'standard' petals carefully into position on top of the flower.

on soft foam and draw the leaf aid tool from the petal ends to the centre, then pull all the petals forward to the same level. Paint the centre of the fall petals with egg white, lift the standards on a cocktail stick (blunt end in the petals) and push into position, alternating with the fall petals. A little egg white on the inside tips of the standards will keep them upright.

LEAVES

5 (For full instructions on making and colouring leaves, see pages 62–5.) The real flower grows up out of the group of leaves, but it is easier just to place the flower stalk behind. Make the green leaves with 24-gauge green wires and the dead leaves with 30-gauge.

6 Work some green flowerpaste to the stage where it is rolled out and stuck to the board, with the wire pointing away from you. Cut out one of the leaf shapes freehand (see page 126), varying this each time you cut out a group. Start by cutting out the longest leaf, which has the wire in it as the main support. Mark continuation lines of leaves in the centre. Let some leaves flop into a natural curve. Make some single, long, curved leaves, and also cut out some small and large twisted single (dead) leaves from beige flowerpaste.

7 Colour the green leaves with Eucalyptus or Eau-de-nil dusting powder, using Baby Maize on the tips and Iris where the leaves grow out of each other. Dust the beige leaves with Pistachio and Oak.

BUDS

8 Cut and hook 4cm (1½in) lengths of 30-gauge white wire. Dip in egg white and pull through a small blob of coloured flowerpaste. Roll out some more paste very thinly, then roll again to texture with lines: use a cocktail stick, or press into corn-on-the-cob husk. Cut out a small rectangle from this paste and thin the edges with a cocktail stick. Paint the non-textured surface with egg white and wrap around the wire at an angle. Remove surplus paste and position the bud below the flower.

9 Repeat step 8 using pale beige paste, and position this slightly lower down on the bud. The base should be very slender so that it can sit close to the main stem.

COLOURING

10 Dust on deeper colours from the petal edges, sometimes leaving the centre much lighter. Use the darkest colour for the buds. Mix Forsythia dusting powder with Paint Aid (see page 10) and paint a little at the centre top of each fall petal.

It is easier to cut out the leaves if you keep the shapes upside down.

Texture the paste for the lower bud with a cocktail stick or corn husk.

Dust the flowers with deeper colours from the edges.

Magnolia

YOU WILL NEED

Cutter Nos 13 and 36

White flowerpaste (gum paste) for first
flower layer and sepals, coloured
with French Pink droplet colour for
second flower layer, pale Christmas
Green paste food colour for flower
centre and leaves, Bamboo droplet
colour for outer flower centre

26- and 24-gauge green wires

30-gauge white wire

Pipe cleaners

Olive florist's tape

Burgundy and Fern droplet colours

Cream or beige dusting powder

Gum arabic solution

Paint Aid

Soft foam

Although the colour of the flowers and number of petals may vary depending on the variety, the basic pattern for magnolia flowers is roughly the same. These impressive blooms can be scaled down in size to make them suitable for cake decoration.

FLOWER CENTRE

1 Tape together two 10cm (4in) lengths of 24-gauge green wire with florist's tape and hook the ends. Form a sausage about 2cm (¾in) long from pale green flowerpaste (gum paste), dip the wire in egg white and pull through.

2 Using fine scissors, snip the paste on the upper three-quarters of the shape, keeping the cuts long but narrow. Try to make these cuts irregular, to avoid lines developing.

3 Cut out two shapes from beige flowerpaste using the No. 36 cutter. Cut each petal in half, then curve on soft foam. Paint the shapes with egg white and position onto the base of the green centre, then paint immediately with Burgundy droplet colour, before the paste dries.

4 Paint the 'snips' with Paint Aid and cream or beige dusting powder. Put on one side to dry. Tape a pipe cleaner to the wires with florist's tape to provide bulk that is easy to cut with wire cutters.

FLOWER

5 Roll out enough white and pink flowerpaste for two petal shapes. Place the white paste on top of the pink. The white paste should be a fraction thicker than the pink so that more white comes through on the

Cut out two shapes for the flower
centre and then cut each petal in half.

Shape the magnolia petals in stages,
using a cocktail stick.

Paint the base of the petal shape with
egg white and wrap around the centre.

back of the petals. Cut out the shapes using the No. 13 cutter. Place one shape on a lightly greased board, keeping the other covered, and cut the petals to points using a palette knife. Using the pointed end of a cocktail stick, work the shape back out, working half the petal at a time. Thin down and spread the bottom triangle as well. You may now need to cut a little further down in between each petal. When you are happy with the shape, paint egg white onto the bottom triangle and wrap it around the prepared centre. Hang upside down to dry.

6 Take the second shape and cut down between to produce three individual petals. Keep two under cover while you work on the other one. Cut this to a point and then work out the paste on a lightly greased board to the same shape as the first three petals. Paint on egg white and fix onto the flower in the space between two petals. Hang upside down between working

petals. Continue with each petal in the same way. When all the petals are in position, support until dry on soft foam in which you have cut a hole with sloping sides.

SEPALS

7 Make three sepals from white flowerpaste and with 30-gauge white wires, following the instructions for making the leaves (see step 8). Cut them out freehand (see page 126), making them about 3cm (1¼in) long and 1cm (½in) wide, and keeping them a little shorter than the petals. Turn the shapes over, curve the sepals a little and distress the edges by

cutting out small, rough-edged pieces. Allow to dry.

LEAVES

8 (For full instructions on making and colouring leaves, see pages 62–5.) Make the leaves with 26-gauge green wires. Cut them out freehand (see page 126) from pale green flowerpaste, varying the sizes from large to small. Curve the sides backwards gently and indent the main vein well with a leaf aid tool. When the leaves are dry, cover the wires with quarter-width florist's tape, then paint the leaves with Fern droplet colour and gum arabic solution.

ASSEMBLY

9 Tape the sepals in position, alternating them with the three final petals. Cover the whole stem with full-width tape. When taping the leaves into place, bring them together in groups of three, leaving a stem for each leaf, and then tape the stem of these three into the main stem. (The lengths of these stems are optional, within reason.)

Support the flower in soft foam, placing it in a hole with sloping sides.

Cut out the sepals freehand, making sure they are slightly shorter than the petals.

Tape the sepals in position, alternating them with the three final petals.

Mock orange blossom

Cutter Nos 4 and 5

White flowerpaste (gum paste) for
flowers and buds about to open,
coloured with Christmas Green paste
food colour for smaller buds, leaves
and flower calyx, pale Christmas
Green for bud calyx

28-, 26- and 24-gauge green wires

Yellow-tipped stamens

White and nile green florist's tape

Euphorbia dusting powder

Fern and Holly Leaf droplet colours

Gum arabic solution

Soft foam

Ripple foam

There are many different varieties of *Philadelphus*, or mock orange.
The one I have chosen to copy is not too large, with no markings
on the petals and the pistil hidden in the freshly opened flower.
A group of three flowers and/or buds at the end of the stem is
followed by two growing from the same point as the pair of leaves.

STAMENS

1 For each flower, take 12 yellow-tipped stamens and cut them in half
to produce 24 stamens per flower,
then trim to about 1.5cm (⅝in) long.
Cut a 8cm (3in) length of 26-gauge
green wire and tape on the stamens
at one end with half-width white
florist's tape. Then cover most of the
white tape with nile green tape right
down to the bottom of the wire,
leaving about 5mm (¼in) of white
tape uncovered at the top. The
stamens need only be showing by
about 5mm (¼in) above the end of
the wire. It is better to have them too
short than too long.

FLOWERS

2 Flatten a marble-sized ball of white
flowerpaste (gum paste) and pinch
around the edge. Roll out the paste
on a lightly greased board, leaving a
very small pimple in the middle. Cut
out the petal shape using the No. 5
cutter, and work the petals with a
blunt cocktail stick until the required
shape is achieved. Work from the
centre of the petal outwards each
time, leaving the centre top edge,
to achieve a slight point. Once all the
petals have been worked, curve them
inwards on soft foam and then place
the flower on ripple foam while you
make the calyx.

Cut the stamens in half to produce
24 per flower and tape to the wire.

Cut out the petal shapes from white
paste and the calyx from green.

Push the flower up the wire and
position at the base of the stamens.

CALYX

3 Cut out a calyx shape from green flowerpaste using the No. 4 cutter. Place the shape on soft foam, curve each sepal with a dogbone tool and paint with egg white. Paint the taped wire below the stamens with egg white as well and pull the stamens through the flower head, then position the calyx behind the flower so that the sepals lie in between the petals. Place a small blob of the same green paste just below the calyx. Dust a slightly darker edging on the sepals with Euphorbia powder.

BUDS

4 Cut a 5cm (2in) length of 28-gauge green wire, hook the end and dip it in egg white. Work a small piece of white flowerpaste into an egg shape about 5mm (¼in) long and pull the hooked wire through. Work the shape further until it comes to a slight point and then indent four times from the point to the base, using a craft knife. Cut out the calyx shape from pale green paste using the No. 4 cutter and curve the sepals. (If you have time, roll out each sepal with a cocktail stick on a lightly greased board until it is very thin, then re-cut the shape with a craft knife. The centre is left untouched, but the sepals will be incredibly thin.) Paint the inside of the calyx with egg white and place on the bud, then fix a small oval of pale green paste behind the calyx as for the flower (see step 3). Make smaller buds from green flowerpaste following exactly the same method.

LEAVES

5 (For full instructions on making and colouring leaves, see pages 62–5.) Make the leaves with 28-gauge green wires. Cut out a number of leaf shapes freehand (see page 126) from green flowerpaste and indent the main vein well using a palette knife. When the paste is dry, paint the whole leaf with Fern droplet colour and gum arabic solution, then use Holly Leaf droplet colour to paint in the shading.

ASSEMBLY

6 Tape three flowers/buds together using half-width nile green florist's tape, allowing a stem about 3cm (1¼in) long for each. Tape in a length of 24-gauge wire to provide extra strength. Leave a space of 3–4cm (1¼–1½in) along the stem and then attach two flowers/buds, with a leaf behind each.

Position the delicate, pale green calyx close to the bud.

Fix a small oval of the same pale green paste behind the calyx.

Tape the flowers, buds and leaves to the stem, strengthened with extra wire.

Open rose

YOU WILL NEED

Cutter Nos 2 and 32

White flowerpaste (gum paste) for
flower, coloured with Christmas
green paste food colour for stamen
centre, calyx and leaves

28- and 24-gauge green wires

30-gauge white wire

Olive florist's tape

Cream or pale green cotton thread

Forsythia and pink dusting powders

Fern droplet colour

Gum arabic solution

Soft foam

One section cut from an egg tray

Once the technique is mastered, these roses can be made up very
easily. Make plenty of buds, open flowers and a few dead heads
from which the petals have fallen, leaving just the stamens and
calyx. Add lots of leaves and cascade the spray over the cake.

STAMENS

1 Make the stamens following the
instructions on page 10, winding the
thread around your fingers about
30 times and using two 8cm (3in)
lengths of 30-gauge white wire. Join
in two 24-gauge green wires at the
base of the threads and tape all the
wires together with half-width
florist's tape. Dip the threads in egg
white, making sure they are well
soaked, and leave to dry overnight.

2 Pull the dried threads well down
with tweezers, bending them as you
go. Brush the ends with egg white,
then dip in Forsythia dusting powder.
Paint some egg white in the middle
of the stamens and push a tiny ball of

pale green flowerpaste (gum paste)
firmly into the middle.

FLOWER

3 Roll out some white flowerpaste
to just under 1mm ($^1/_{16}$in) thick and
cut out the petal shape using the
No. 2 cutter. Place the shape near
the edge of a lightly greased board.
With each petal in turn, roll out the
paste on either side of the centre
heart shape, using the sharp end
of a cocktail stick. Using a rocking
action, with most pressure applied
to the shoulder of the cocktail stick,
swell out the paste until it makes a
rounded heart shape. You will need
to re-position the cocktail stick after
each rocking action, so that a fan

Make the stamens from cotton thread,
dipped in Forsythia dusting powder.

Curl the petals on soft foam, using the
small end of a leaf aid tool.

Place the calyx over the flower shape
while it is on the section of egg box.

shape is achieved. This technique texture the petals as well as enabling you to produce extremely fine paste around the edges, leaving the paste in the middle the original thickness.

4 Place the petal shape on soft foam and curl the petals with the small end of a leaf aid tool. To do this, push the tool under one petal to reach one half of the next. Place the tool diagonally across the petal and gently pull into the centre. Curl one side of each petal of the whole flower, then reverse the action for the other side. This may take a little practice.

5 Put the section of egg tray in the centre of the petal shape and turn upside down. Leave to rest while you cut out the calyx.

CALYX

6 Roll out some green flowerpaste very thinly and cut out a calyx shape using the No. 32 cutter. Thin down the edges using a cocktail stick, re-cut the points if necessary and cut the sides as shown opposite and on page 53. Paint the centre with egg white and place carefully over the

flower shape so that the sepals are behind the petals.

7 Paint egg white behind the stamens, and make a very small round shape from green flowerpaste ready to position behind the calyx.

8 Gently tip the flower shape, with its calyx, onto your hand, then twist through the wire plus stamens and pull into place. Slide the small round piece of paste up the wire until it is firmly positioned behind the calyx. Hang the flower upside down, especially if you want it half open.

LEAVES

9 (For full instructions on making and colouring leaves, see pages

62–5.) Use 28-gauge green wires to make the leaves, cutting them out freehand (see page 126) from green flowerpaste. There are generally three leaves in the group just behind the flower, then at least five in the other groups: use the largest at the top, and then matching pairs that get smaller as you go down the stems, at intervals of about 2cm (¾in).

10 To make a stipule for the base of the leaf stem, roll out some green flowerpaste very thinly on a lightly greased board and cut out the shape shown on page 126. Paint the wire with egg white and press the stipule firmly into position at the base using a cocktail stick.

COLOURING

11 Allow the flowers to dry and then dust the backs of the petals with pink. Some of the colour will show through. For the half-open flower, a little dusting powder may be needed on the upper surface of the petals to make the whole flower darker.

12 Paint the leaves with Fern droplet colour and gum arabic solution, then dust a little pink powder onto the edges while the paint is still tacky.

Press the stipule firmly into position using a cocktail stick.

Dust the backs of the petals with pink dusting powder.

Pansy

Cutter Nos 6 (or 33), 18–21, 22, 29 and 39

Flowerpaste (gum paste) coloured with Melon paste food colour or Royal Blue droplet colour for flowers and buds, Christmas Green for calyx and leaves

28- and 26-gauge green wires

Nile green or olive florist's tape

Yellow stamens

Dusting powders in suitable colours

Fern and Burgundy (optional) droplet colours

Gum arabic solution

Paint Aid

Soft foam

Colour shaper (optional)

We are lucky to be able to enjoy this well-loved flower for most of the year. With the introduction of many new varieties, the colours, too, are almost limitless. It is perhaps the little 'faces' which give pansies so much charm, but they can also be plain with no markings.

FLOWER

1 Tape together two 9–10cm (3½–4in) lengths of 26-gauge green wire with florist's tape and hook one end. Form a round pad of coloured flowerpaste (gum paste), slightly smaller than the No. 18 cutter. Pull up a column (the throat) in the centre, then lay the paste on a lightly greased board and roll out all the way around with a Leicester tool until fairly thin. Make sure there is very little thickness at the base of the throat. Using the No. 18 (or 19, 20 or 21) cutter, cut out the petal shape.

2 Almost overlap two of the petals and press them together (to make the large bottom petal). Using a blunt cocktail stick, start from the centre of the joined petals and roll outwards until the paste reaches the next side petal. Repeat on the other side.

3 Working on one at a time, roll out the two side petals until they are more than double their original size. Move the lower edge of the petals behind the large one. Finally, thin down the two top petals and then put the lower edge of each petal behind the side ones.

4 Pick up the shape from the board, then open up the throat with the pointed end of the cocktail stick and 'lean' against each of the petals in turn. Make an indentation on the paste from the base of the petals in towards the centre with a leaf aid tool, to give the impression that they are all separate, right into the throat.

5 Using blunt tweezers, pinch the paste into a ridge at the base of the two side petals. Place the flower on soft foam and curve the side of the

Retaining the central column, shape the petals in several stages.

Curve the side of the large bottom petal diagonally with a leaf aid tool.

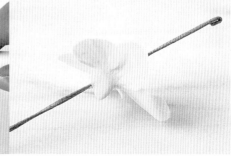

Push the hooked wire up the flower throat (hook towards the bottom petal).

large bottom petal diagonally with a leaf aid tool. Curve the two side petals back on themselves, then bring them forward on both sides of the flower. Make sure the top petals do not drop backwards.

6 Dip the hooked wire into egg white and then push it up the throat of the flower, with the hook facing towards the large bottom petal. When the wire is in place, pinch the paste from the back. Cut off the head of a yellow stamen and push it into the throat so that it is resting on the base of the large petal (the entrance to the throat).

7 With the flower facing you, hold the wire firmly just behind the flower head with tweezers and then bend the wire downwards using your other hand.

CALYX
8 When the flower is dry, cut out a calyx from green flowerpaste, using a No. 6 or No. 33 cutter. Cut slightly into the shape to open it out, place it on the soft foam and curve the sepals backwards. Pick up the calyx, paint

egg white on the other side and then slide it onto the back of the flower, with the cut sitting over the position where the wire emerges.

9 Cut out a calyx shape from green flowerpaste using the No. 22 cutter. Curve this and paint the middle of the underside with egg white. Slide into place on the calyx (it is part of the same structure). Bend the little lobes back and pinch into place.

COLOURING
10 When the flowers are dry, paint with Paint Aid and a suitable powder colour (see page 10), to produce a velvet effect. If you want lines on the petals, paint them very neatly with Burgundy droplet colour.

11 If you have painted the petal edges only, take a dry, clean paintbrush and some dry dusting powder and gently dust from the edge and a little way into the centre, to soften any hard edges.

BUDS
12 Make a slender cone about 1cm (½in) long from coloured flowerpaste.

Cut and hook a 5cm (2in) length of 28-gauge green wire and pull through the cone. Cut out a petal shape using the No. 39 cutter, thin down the edges, paint with egg white and fix in position over the cone, like a little bonnet. Make and add a calyx in the same way as for the flower (see steps 8 and 9).

LEAVES
13 Follow the instructions on page 67. When dry, tape at least three leaves together, each with a little stalk, then tape the combined stem to the base of the flower stem.

At the base of the two side petals, pinch the paste into a ridge.

Fix the second part of the calyx in position and bend back the little lobes.

Paint the flower with Paint Aid and powder colour, for a velvet finish.

Rose

When making roses, I work with two different-coloured pastes, placed one on top of the other and then rolled together. Even when making a white rose it is better to have a slightly coloured paste underneath, as this produces a realistic shaded effect.

YOU WILL NEED

Cutter Nos 14 and 32
Flowerpaste (gum paste) in two
   colours of your choice for flower,
   Christmas Green paste food colour
   for calyx
Leftover flowerpaste for flower centre
24-gauge green wire
Olive florist's tape
Soft foam

FLOWER

1 If you are making a number of roses of the same colour, make up a large lump of each of the two coloured flowerpastes (gum pastes), then work with just enough to make one flower at a time. Any surplus paste can be kneaded together to make flowers that will blend well with the original choice.

2 Tape together two 9cm (3½in) lengths of 24-gauge green wire with florist's tape and hook one end. Dip in egg white and fix into a pointed blob of leftover flowerpaste. The size should be within the length of the petal part of the No. 14 cutter. Allow to dry at least overnight.

3 Roll the two flowerpastes for the petals together, then cut out five petal shapes (one extra in case of mistakes). Place one shape on the edge of a lightly greased board. Starting on the left-hand side (if you are right-handed), press the paste down to make it stick to the board. Using a blunt cocktail stick, start from the centre and thin down the paste with a rocking action, then go back to the centre and repeat outwards to the other side. Control the pressure on the cocktail stick with the index finger of your other hand. The aim is to create the shape of the conventional rose petal, which by this time should be two to three times the original size. Fold this over and work the second petal in the same way, then the third petal. Grease the board again after each complete shape has been worked.

4 Dip the dried centre in egg white. With every shape, paint egg white

Make the flower centre and then cut and shape the petals in stages.

Wrap the first petal shape tightly around the flower centre and tuck in the petals.

Remove any surplus paste underneath the flower with your fingers.

on the bottom triangle as well as on the petals, even though it is removed eventually. With the first shape, bring the middle petal forward and paint with egg white completely. Wrap this petal around the rose centre, making sure it is wrapped tightly. Paint egg white almost to the top of the remaining two petals and stick the left-hand side of the right-hand one to the centre, then bring the left-hand petal forward, turn it around, and stick the right-hand side to the front. Now wrap these two around – they should tuck inside each other. Take off surplus paste underneath with your fingers. You can add a calyx at this stage to form a tight bud.

5 Work the second shape in the same way as the first (see step 3). Paint egg white about one-third of the way up the petals, and then wrap around the bud. Turn the edges of the petals over, using a cocktail stick to curve the paste. Work with the flower on a flower pad so that you have both hands free to curve the petals. Take off the surplus paste underneath with your fingers.

6 Work the third shape in the same way as the first two (see step 3). Paint on egg white one-third of the way up, wrap around the flower and turn down the petals (see step 5). This should wrap roughly three-quarters of the way around the flower.

7 Cut one petal off the last shape. Work and paint with egg white as before (see steps 3 and 5) and place in the gap. Trim away surplus paste from the last two shapes with your fingers. Throughout, hold the wire between your thumb and third finger, which then allows you to model with your two index fingers and the thumb of your other hand.

CALYX
8 Cut out the calyx from green flowerpaste using the No. 32 cutter and cut the edges of some of the sepals as shown on the shape on page 126 and below right. Place the calyx on soft foam and curl the sepals with a dogbone tool. Paint the inside with

egg white, then slide the calyx up the wire and into position at the back of the rose. Form a small oval shape from the same green flowerpaste. Dent one end with the blunt end of a cocktail stick, paint with egg white, then slide this up the wire and position it directly below the calyx.

LEAVES
9 There is usually a group of three leaves about 6cm (2½in) below the flower head, and then groups of five leaves at similar intervals below that. For full instructions on making the leaves, see steps 9 and 10 on page 49.

Turn the petals over, curving the paste with a cocktail stick.

Model the petals with your fingers to achieve the characteristic rose shape.

Cut out the calyx and then cut into the edges of some of the sepals.

Scabious

This well-loved, showy flower is ideal to use on cakes for summer events, as the lovely mauve shades, especially alongside lemon and white, create a very refreshing picture. You can, of course, vary the colours to suit your scheme.

Calyx

1 Tape together three 8cm (3in) 24-gauge green wires with florist's tape, leaving about 5mm (¼in) free at the top. Splay out these wires. Cut out two shapes from green flowerpaste (gum paste) using the No. 35 cutter. Turn both shapes over and paint with egg white. Place the stem on one shape, adjusting the angle of the wires if necessary, then slide the second shape up the stem to meet the first. Working on a board, adjust the shapes so that they are neatly stuck together, hiding the wires. Dry upside down. Fix a small domed pad of the same green flowerpaste in the centre of the calyx with egg white. It should be about 2.5mm (⅛in) thick in the middle and should not extend over the sepals.

Flower

2 Roll out the mauve flowerpaste and dust with Platinum Lilac dusting powder, then cut out eight shapes using the No. 3 cutter. Place one shape on the edge of a lightly greased board. Using the blunt end of a cocktail stick, spread each petal until really thin. If you are right-handed, thin the left-hand lobe of the three first. Once thinned, fold it out of the way and then work on the next petal, until all three have been thinned. Then work just on the edge of each petal to frill it, using the shoulder of the cocktail stick. On the central

Cut out the calyx from green paste, fix onto splayed wire and add a centre pad.

Shape and frill the petals, flipping each one out of the way to work the others.

As you fix the petals in place, make sure the side ones are brought forward.

petal, thin down the edges only, frill the edge of the end, and paint egg white across the base. Fold the petal in half, stick down either side and lift up the centre with the point of the cocktail stick to form a pocket. Cut off the corners of this petal using the pointed end of the cocktail stick.

3 Paint egg white onto one sepal at a time and then fix each shape onto the calyx as it is worked, lifting it off the board using the sharp end of a cocktail stick.

4 Place some sago and Dark Eucalyptus dusting powder in a small jar with a lid, and give it a shake. Mix some green flowerpaste with plenty of egg white to make a thick paste. Smear this over the domed centre of the flower and then place the coloured sago all over it, using tweezers to hold the little pieces.

LEAVES
5 (For full instructions on making and colouring leaves, see pages 62–5.) Make the leaves with 28-gauge green wires. Foliage shapes for the various types of scabious differ

markedly. The simple shape can be cut out freehand, but for the others use the No. 38 cutter or press the real leaf onto the paste. When the leaves are dry, paint with Fern droplet colour and gum arabic solution.

COLOURING
6 Dust the edges of the petals very carefully with African Violet powder, and also put a little of this colour into the centre of the flower.

(The tiny pieces in the middle open up as the flower matures, but it would be very time consuming to reproduce this. I would not attempt the wild scabious because of the large centre full of these tiny florets, nor would I try to make the buds of either wild or cultivated scabious, as they are very complicated and could look heavy unless expertly done.) Dust the petals further with Mauve Mist powder.

Use a cocktail stick to lift and position the petals one by one on the calyx.

Place coloured sago in the middle of the flower, to represent the central florets.

Dust the petals with African Violet and Mauve Mist dusting powders.

Snowdrop

It is easier to copy the single snowdrop, as the double version has so many petals that it would be difficult to give the true impression of daintiness. You may find it easier to paint the green markings on the first petal shape before adding the sepals.

FLOWER

1 Cut a 9cm (3½in) length of 26-gauge green wire and hook the end. Dip in egg white and pull through a small piece of white flowerpaste (gum paste) – this should be small enough to sit inside the petals to give them shape but not show. Push in three 5mm (¼in) lengths of yellow stamen thread and allow to dry.

2 Roll out some white flowerpaste quite thinly and then cut out shapes for the heart-shaped and pointed petals, using the Nos 7 and 8 cutters. Take the heart-shaped petals and thin down just the edges by applying pressure with a cocktail stick along the full length. Turn the shape over, place it on soft foam, and curl the petals by drawing a dogbone tool from the outer edge of the shape towards the centre.

3 Paint egg white on the flower centre and then pull the wire through the prepared petal shape until the centre is settled in position. Make sure that the petals tuck inside each other.

4 Thin down the edges of the pointed petals and curl them inwards, using the cocktail stick and dogbone tool in exactly the same way as you did for the heart-shaped petals on the first layer (see step 2). Paint the centre of the petal shape with egg white and position it

The heart-shaped inner petals should tuck inside each other.

Paint the green markings on the inner petals with Fern droplet colour.

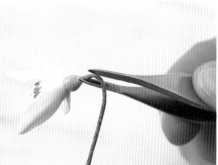

Using tweezers, curve the stem just behind the flower head.

behind the first layer, taking care to alternate the positions of the petals on the two layers.

5 Form a small oval shape from green flowerpaste. Dent one end with the blunt end of the cocktail stick, paint on a little egg white and slide the shape into position at the back of the flower. Cover the stem with half-width florist's tape, then curve it over gently just behind the flower head.

SPATHE

6 Make a long, very thin sausage from green flowerpaste for the spathe. Place it on a lightly greased board, lay the pointed end of the cocktail stick down the full length and press with a slight rocking motion. This will create two thicker rolls of paste with a very thin section in the middle. Cut to about 2cm (¾in) long, paint egg white on the blunt end and then place the flower wire on this (which is easier than trying to pick up the paste and position it with your fingers). The spathe should be positioned just below the curve of the wire. Bend the green flowerpaste into a gentle curve: a real snowdrop spathe can actually be quite straight, but this would look very stiff reproduced in flowerpaste and could be knocked off too easily.

COLOURING

7 When dry, paint markings on the inner petals with Fern droplet colour as shown in the shape on page 124. There are other markings for different varieties, for which you can consult good gardening books.

LEAVES

8 (For full instructions on making and colouring leaves, see pages 62–5.) Make the leaves with 28-gauge green wires. Working freehand, cut out a number of very narrow leaves (see page 124) and round the points by working them with a cocktail stick. Gently curve most of the leaves, but leave a few almost straight. Snowdrop leaves are generally a dark blue-green colour on both sides with a lighter tip. When dry, paint with Holly Leaf droplet colour with a little Dark Eucalyptus powder mixed in, plus gum arabic solution.

ASSEMBLY

9 In their natural state, when snowdrop flowers are fully open they will be above the level of the leaves. To make arranging easier, tape two or three leaves to the base of the flower stem first.

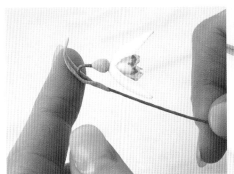

Make the spathe from green paste and fix it just below the curve of the stem.

Round the points of the leaves using pressure on a cocktail stick.

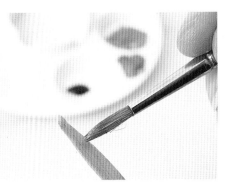

Paint the leaves with Holly Leaf and Dark Eucalyptus colour, plus gum arabic.

Tulip

YOU WILL NEED

Cutter No. 17

Flowerpaste (gum paste) coloured
   with colour of your choice for flower,
   very pale Christmas Green paste
   food colour for pistil, Christmas
   Green for leaves

26- and 24-gauge green wires

30-gauge white wire

Pipe cleaners

Scientific wire

White and nile green florist's tape

Yellow, burgundy or brown florist's
   tape for stamens

Euphorbia dusting powder, plus
   colour(s) of your choice

Soft foam

This method will enable you to make tulips more easily than trying to assemble six separate petals with difficult curves. Copy varieties with slightly more pointed petals until you are experienced in the technique. When the flower is just opening the inside petals often remain quite tightly closed, making it a lot easier to copy.

STAMENS AND PISTIL

1 Pull on a length of scientific wire to straighten it. Wrap short lengths of yellow, burgundy or brown florist's tape onto the wire at 2.5cm (1in) intervals, then use wire cutters to cut the wire at one end of each length of tape to produce the stamens. Roll the end of the stamens in your fingers to get rid of the cut flat end.

2 For the pistil, roll some very pale green flowerpaste (gum paste) into a narrow sausage. Cut a 4cm (1½in) length of 30-gauge white wire, dip in egg white and pull through the paste, but leave the wire along the full length of the sausage. Roll the paste on your hand, squashing it to just below the end and trim away the excess. Push the paste down on the end to form a thicker pad and then divide it by indenting three times with the hook of a leaf aid tool. Curve the length slightly to make it equal to or slightly shorter than the stamens. Using full-width white florist's tape, tape six stamens and the pistil to two 10cm (4in) lengths of 24-gauge green wire, together with a pipe cleaner, centring the pistil. Trim away excess pipe cleaner if necessary.

FLOWER

3 Make a fat cone from coloured flowerpaste, about the same length as the finished flower size. Cut into the cone three times with a fine palette knife, from the point downwards for about three-quarters of the length. Push fine scissors into the cuts to make three petals which open up only part of the cone. Push in the pointed end of a cocktail stick and,

Cut at one end of the taped wire for each stamen, using wire cutters.

Shape the pistil with your fingers, then indent with the hook of a leaf aid tool.

Tape six stamens and the pistil to two lengths of wire, plus a pipe cleaner.

treating each petal as two halves, roll the paste against your index finger until it is thin. You may need to trim with scissors as you work, to achieve the shape you want. Curl the edges of the petals using either the cocktail stick against your finger or a leaf aid tool on soft foam. To achieve the very rounded shape on the finished flower you must take care at this stage, as the shape of the bottom of the cone will determine the final character of the flower.

4 Paint the stem immediately under the stamens with egg white, then pull the wire down through the flower until the stamens are well inside. Check that the shape is still neat and rounded, trimming off any surplus paste with your fingers. Hang upside down and allow to dry overnight. When dry, dust on the required colour, not necessarily down to the stalk as there is often a fading or change of colour.

5 Roll out some coloured flowerpaste, not too thinly, and cut out three petals using the No. 17 cutter. They should be 1cm (½in)

longer than the cone. Working on a lightly greased board, use the cocktail stick to thin down and spread the paste at the pointed end until you have the same shape as on the inside petals. Place the petal on soft foam and curl the top edges slightly using the leaf aid tool. Paint egg white onto the lower part of the dried centre and fix the petal firmly in place. Continue in the same way with the other two petals, overlapping them as you go. If necessary, hang the completed flower upside down to dry, then colour to match the inside petals (see step 4).

Leaves

6 (For full instructions on making leaves, see pages 62–4.) It is essential to remember to make the curve of the leaves. The first couple that are positioned around the flower head, growing from the stalk, may need a curve across the width as well as the full length. The leaf nearest the

flower should be the shortest. Make the leaves with 26-gauge green wires. Cut out a number of leaves in varying sizes freehand (see page 126) from pale green flowerpaste. Remember to cut away the small section at the base of the leaf, so that it will sit neatly against the thick stem. Lift the paste off the board, lay it on soft foam and curve the edges inwards with the leaf aid tool. When dry, dust with Euphorbia powder. Tape the leaves to the flower stem with nile green tape – many smaller varieties have leaves all the way down, the first couple high enough up to be level with the flower.

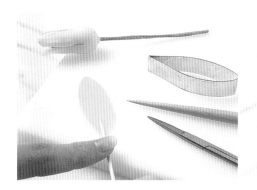

Work the outer petals to the required shape using a cocktail stick.

Fix on the outer petals, overlapping them as you go. Remove surplus paste.

Curve the leaves along their full length, using a leaf aid tool.

White heather

This is a flower for good luck, and not to be confused with sea lavender, which street vendors often sell. Although the stems of the little flowers are actually pale green, I make them on white wires unless I have time to stain some a very pale green.

YOU WILL NEED
No cutter required
White flowerpaste (gum paste) for flowers
26- or 24-gauge green wire
30-gauge white wire
Nile green and beige florist's tape
Fern (optional) and Burgundy or Bamboo droplet colours

FLOWERS
1 Break off tiny pieces of white flowerpaste (gum paste) and form each into a tiny peardrop shape about 2.5mm (⅛in) long. Hollow this out to about half the length and break up the rim slightly using the pointed end of a cocktail stick, against your index finger. Paint in some egg white and thread the flower onto a 12cm (5in) length of 30-gauge white wire. (If preferred, stain the wire with Fern droplet colour, following the instructions on page 6.) Make more flowers, on half-length wires, and pinch each one into place on the wire as you work, positioning them at intervals of about 1.5cm (⅝in).

LEAVES
2 Cut some half- and quarter-width nile green florist's tape into 1.5cm (⅝in) lengths, according to the number of leaves required. Make cuts in one end of all these pieces, to form a group of tiny leaves.

ASSEMBLY
3 Cut the flower stems to about 1mm (¹⁄₁₆in) beyond the white paste of the flower.

4 Cut a 10cm (4in) length of 26- or 24-gauge green wire for the main stem. Tape all the flowers onto the main stem in clusters with half-width beige florist's tape, bringing in the little groups of leaves at intervals. Ensure that all the flowers face the same way.

5 Paint the tiny bit of wire that is sticking out of each of the flowers with Burgundy or Bamboo droplet colour. Finally, put a slight bend into the main stem and flower stems.

Make cuts in one end of several pieces of tape, to form groups of tiny leaves.

Tape the flowers to the main stem in clusters, all facing the same way.

Paint the wire ends with Burgundy or Bamboo droplet colour.

Witch hazel

The flowers of this early spring-flowering shrub are made here mainly from yellow tape and are quick to complete. You can cluster the flowers, but just a few on a twig will also look good.

FLOWERS

1 Cut 1cm (½in) lengths of yellow florist's tape, and then cut these into eighths lengthwise by cutting in half, then half again, and then a final half. Taking one length at a time, put the tape on some hard foam, place the tip of a leaf aid tool on one end and pull the tape through. This will both stretch and stiffen the tape. Take two of these lengths and form a cross with another two.

2 Hook a 4cm (1½in) length of 30-gauge white wire. Form a very small ball of beige flowerpaste (gum paste) into a cone about 5mm (¼in) long and open up the wide end using a cocktail stick. Cut this into four, pinch each to a point, and then thin out with the blunt end of the cocktail stick. Dip the hooked wire in egg white and pull through the cone. Paint straight away with neat Burgundy droplet colour.

3 While the paste and paint are still wet, put in the yellow tape petals. Press the blunt end of a cocktail stick into the middle of the petals, pick them up and press them into the little beige cone.

ASSEMBLY

4 To form the twig, first make the growing tip. Cut a 2.5cm (1in) length of nile green or beige florist's tape. Roll half of this, then double it over and squeeze together, making sure you leave half the length for fixing it to the wire. Cut a 10cm (4in) length of 24-gauge green wire, fix on the growing tip and then cover the wire right to the end with half-width beige florist's tape. Tape on one flower 2.5–4cm (1–1½in) from the top of the twig. Then fix on more flowers down the twig, clustering two or three fairly haphazardly at each point. There are no leaves present when the shrub is in flower.

Stretch and stiffen the tape for the petals by pulling it under a leaf aid tool.

Paint the central cone with Burgundy droplet colour before adding the petals.

Push the petals into the paste cone, then tape onto the twig.

Leaves

The basic technique for making all leaves is the same (and can also be used to make single petals for flowers such as lilies and nasturtiums). The method is described below, with any variations for particular leaves given in the instructions for the relevant project.

For all leaves that you wish to make, it is a good idea to photocopy the real leaf for future reference. If appropriate, leave the stalk on to serve as a reminder of the way it grows.

WIRES

Cut the wires ready before you start making the leaves. The gauge required will vary, as it depends on several factors. These include leaf size (larger leaves need a heavier gauge), whether or not the leaf requires support at the tip and may need to bend (possibly a lighter gauge), and where many small leaves are being taped together (use a light gauge for each). For example, in the latter case you could use 30- or 32-gauge wires; or, if the leaf is large and has a stalk (petiole) a 24-gauge wire would be appropriate.

Keep the wires straight at all times and discard any lengths that are badly bent. Always cut off about 2.5mm ($^1/_8$in) from both ends of a new wire, as they are often rough and this would tear the paste.

When assembling several leaves onto a stem, as with roses for example, cover the end leaf wire with quarter-width florist's tape.

When you bring in the side leaves, tape them to the centre wire and carefully pull on each of the side wires in turn in order to bring them in neatly with very little stalk.

PREPARING THE PASTE

1 Form a sausage from flowerpaste (gum paste) by rolling it on the palm of your hand, usually with three fingers. Take a wire, dip it in egg white and then push the dry end through the paste and pull until the wet end is inside. Again roll the paste on the palm of your hand, wire pointing away from you, taking a little extra care at both ends to make the shape pointed. The wire will now be well embedded in the paste.

2 Lightly grease a board just in the corner where you are going to work. Lay the paste on the board so that the wire is pointing away from you. Place your third finger on the wire to prevent it from moving around and flatten the paste with a thin palette knife by pressing down with the index finger of both hands. Now roll out the paste again with a wooden tool such as a Leicester tool, as wood does not give in the same way as

plastic. You may need to repeat the whole process several times, as each time the palette knife presses down you will probably see a thicker area of paste on either side of the wire, although on larger areas of leaves and petals this may be needed as added support so you may not need to thin down quite as much as on a smaller leaf. The thinner you can make the paste, especially on the edges, the more you will be able to model it.

3 For most leaves, the wire need only project into the leaf shape for about one-quarter of the overall length. Locate the end of the wire before starting to cut out the leaf, perhaps marking the side of the paste to indicate where it is.

TIP
Whenever you need to lift the paste off the board, start by raising it with a palette knife from the wire end.

CUTTING OUT
FREEHAND
If you are cutting out the leaf shape freehand, the paste must be stuck to

the board. Use a craft knife and keep it as upright as possible, for ease and speed of cutting. For long leaves such as those of daffodils and snowdrops, it can be easier to use a thin palette knife for cutting.

CUTTER

If you are using a cutter, check that it has a piece of metal cut away so that there will be no pressure on the wire. Roll out the paste thinly, then lift it off the board with a palette knife and re-position on a dry area of the board ready to cut out the required shape. I use cutters for numerous standard leaf shapes such as holly, ivy, chrysanthemum and alchemilla.

REAL LEAVES

Real leaves, such as alexanders (see page 118), can be used as a template as long as they are neither too soft nor very fleshy. Work the paste to the stage where it is stuck to the board, press the back of the real leaf onto the paste and then lift it off – in most cases, it will have left a very clear outline. Keep the leaf to hand for reference as you work in case any part has not come out well. Now cut along the outline, holding the craft knife as upright as possible.

The real leaf can often be preserved for future use with the following method, but you will need to remove any stalk.

1 Cover a piece of card (I usually use the side of a cereal box) with wide double-sided adhesive tape. Remove the backing paper but keep some to hand. Place the dry leaf on the sticky surface, sticking down from the point towards the stalk.

2 Place a craft cutting board or very thick card underneath, ready to cut out around the leaf. It is a good idea to cut strips of the adhesive tape backing paper to put back around the leaf, as you need to hold the card steady while you cut and if you have been pressing down on the sticky surface it can be very painful when you try to pull your fingers away!

3 Cut out around the leaf with a craft knife, taking your time as you do not want to damage it.

If there is a bulky stem and the flowerpaste leaf is to be taped onto the stem without a stalk, cut out a small half-moon section at the base of the leaf so that it will fit snugly when the plant is assembled.

VEINING AND CURVING
MAIN VEIN

Most leaves have a well-defined main vein. To mark this in, lift the leaf shape from the board, turn it over and lay it on soft foam, then indent the vein either with a thin palette knife or, for a less well-marked line (as on a petal), a leaf aid tool.

Scabious   *Sycamore*

SIDE VEINS

Side veins can be made easily using the hook at the end of the leaf aid tool. Line up the tip with the main vein and then roll the tool back towards the edge of the leaf.

CURVING

Any curving of leaves can be done with a leaf aid tool. Place the leaf on soft foam and stroke the leaf aid tool from the edge towards the main vein – do this on the back to get the edges curving back, as for older leaves, or on the top surface, especially near the stalk, for a forwards curl. The thinner the paste in the final stages, the easier it will be to curve the edges softly and model the shape.

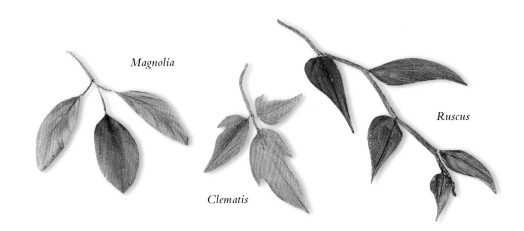

Magnolia

Ruscus

Clematis

DRYING

Most leaves will be dry enough after shaping to push into a block of polystyrene, but should be left to dry thoroughly before painting, dusting or assembly. Push the leaf wires into the block at an angle, placing them so that they will not go on bending when you are not looking.

Conditions of paste, atmosphere and so on will vary, so you may need to hang the newly made leaves to dry briefly from a polystyrene block placed at the edge of a table, pushing the wires into the bottom of the block. Use this method for petals, too.

Alternatively, rest the leaves on ripple foam, but make sure that the shaping is not disturbed.

EDGES

Use a serrator (see page 68) for the edges of rose, cyclamen and other leaves where a really fine-toothed edge is required.

LARGER TOOTHED EDGE

For a toothed edge such as that found on the leaves of marguerite, hops and acers, the following method needs a little practice but certainly gets results.

Drying leaves

1 Prepare the leaf to the stage where the shape is cut out and is well stuck to the board. Place the blade of a craft knife at a 45-degree angle to the edge of the leaf, and with the blade on the board scrape away less than 1mm (¹⁄₁₆in) from the edge of the leaf. The angle of the blade should always be away from the leaf edge.

2 Work your way around the leaf, making the cuts as close together or as far apart as needed.

> **TIP**
> You can use this method to transform many shapes from your cutters into a different plant, such as changing an ivy into an acer.

LOBED EDGE

If you want a lobed edge, use the method above for a larger toothed edge but make the cuts further apart, then apply pressure on the lobes briefly with the shoulder of a cocktail stick. Work with the leaf face down on the board – for some reason, it looks even better when you finally turn it over.

ROUNDED POINT

For a long leaf with a rounded point such as daffodil, snowdrop or bluebell leaves, cut to a sharp point, and then apply pressure to this area with the shoulder of a cocktail stick to form the rounded shape you require. This is much quicker than trying to cut a rounded end.

LEAF DAMAGE

If you want to reproduce the little damage holes caused by insects, slugs and so on, remember that such creatures usually eat between the veins. Use a craft knife or similar tool to create the holes.

COLOURING

For colouring leaves, I almost always use droplet colours in conjunction with gum arabic solution (see page 11) instead of water or alcohol. For lighter leaves or younger growth, I use Fern droplet colour, with Holly Leaf for older or darker leaves.

1 Make the flowerpaste for the leaf the same colour as the main vein – if you are making variegated leaves, you can colour the paste either cream or pale yellow (see page 10).

2 Place gum arabic solution in one section of a palette and the droplet colour in the next section. Dip a good sable paintbrush size 5 or 6 in the gum arabic solution and take it onto the flat area of the palette, then pick up some of the droplet colour and mix with gum arabic solution to the depth of colour required.

3 Using the same paintbrush, paint the colour from the stalk end of the leaf outwards in one movement. The paint will quickly become tacky, so do not fuss around. As the paste surface was originally next to the greased board, the paint will tend to separate on first application, but if you immediately paint over the area again this effect will disappear.

4 To show the veins, remove the paint from the vein area of the leaf as soon as colouring is complete. A

Rosemary

Pittosporum

Variegated holly

colour shaper is a useful tool for this. If you need a coloured edge, dust this straight away with the appropriate colour dusting powder, holding the brush at right angles to the leaf.

> **TIP**
>
> If you need to add any darker colours, such as those on geranium leaves, use colourless alcohol instead of gum arabic solution. I do not generally steam leaves or flowers, but will do so occasionally for dusted autumnal colourings to help blend them. Steaming also helps to fix the colour and prevent it dropping onto the cake surface – in most of the cakes in this book there is a perspex disc underneath the plant arrangement, so this is not a consideration.

VARIEGATED LEAVES
This method can be used to make variegated varieties of holly, ivy, aucuba, daphne and other plants.

1 Make the leaves from pale cream or yellow flowerpaste and allow to dry thoroughly.

2 Melt some vegetable fat (shortening) and paint this onto the dry leaf, feathering it from the edge. If you want spots as well as a cream-coloured edge, paint these on too. Place the leaves in the refrigerator for about ten minutes to set the fat.

3 Paint over the whole surface with the green colour of your choice – the paint will not stick to the areas

covered with vegetable fat. If some of the paint sticks where it is not supposed to, wait until the leaf is dry and then rub gently over the whole surface with your fingers.

FILLER LEAVES, GRASSES AND TWIGS
In addition to the leaves made for the flower projects, for some of the cakes in this book I have included extra foliage to complete the arrangement. The methods for making specific varieties are described below; for some cakes, you can also use any other 'filler foliage' you may have available. Alchemilla leaves and rusty-back fern, which are used on several cakes, are covered in their own projects on pages 68 and 69.

SHAMROCK (CLOVER)
The national emblem of Ireland, this leaf is divided into three, occasionally four (lucky!), leaflets.

1 Tape three 28-gauge green wires together with florist's tape, leaving about 5mm (¼in) free at one end. Splay out the wires.

2 Cut out two shapes from green flowerpaste for each leaf using the No. 8 cutter (see page 63). Turn the paste over and paint egg white on both pieces. Place the splayed wires onto one shape, then pick up the other and slide

it down the wire. Press the two shapes together, enclosing the wires.

3 If the paste looks too thick, thin down with a cocktail stick and re-cut to shape. Lift the leaf off the board and indent through the centre of each part with a leaf aid tool.

4 When dry, paint the top surface with gum arabic solution and Fern droplet colour.

ROSEMARY
Sprigs of this well-known herb, with its small, narrow leaves, make useful filler foliage for arrangements featuring larger leaves of different shapes, such as alchemilla.

1 Cut at least eight 4cm (1½in) lengths of 32-gauge white wire for each sprig.

Aucuba

Shamrock

Rose

Scabious/pansy

2 Using very pale green flowerpaste and following the basic techniques described in this section, make the tiny leaves about 2cm (¾in) long, very narrow and with a rounded point. Vary the sizes of the leaves slightly. Indent the main vein heavily and give each leaf a gentle curve as you work it.

3 Tape the leaves onto 24-gauge white wire with half-width white florist's tape, arranging pairs of leaves facing each other and at right angles to the previous pair. Use the smaller leaves at the top, and progressively larger ones as you work your way down. When assembled, paint the leaves with Holly Leaf droplet colour and gum arabic solution.

EUCALYPTUS
The young foliage of some eucalyptus species can be used to good effect in flower arrangements. When the plant grows older the leaf changes to a long, narrow shape.

1 Make the leaves following the basic techniques described in this section, using 30-gauge green wires. Working freehand and using pale green flowerpaste, cut out a round shape with a tiny point opposite the stem (see page 126).

2 Use a 24-gauge green wire for the main stem. Start with tiny leaves, which will be upright and facing

each other. Tape subsequent pairs at right angles to the previous pair, the leaves getting bigger and less upright as you go down the stem.

3 Dust with Eucalyptus powder and use pink or yellow on the edges, depending on the colour scheme.

PITTOSPORUM
Whether you are making the burgundy-coloured or light green varieties – there are many different kinds – the main feature common to most pittosporums is the wavy edge of the leaf and the dark brown stems. These characteristics make them great favourites with florists and flower arrangers.

1 Make the leaves from pale green flowerpaste cut out freehand (see page 126) following the basic techniques described in this section, then use a dogbone tool on the edge, half on and half off, and apply a little pressure to achieve the movement so characteristic of these leaves. To do this, put the leaf on your hand or on hard foam and pull the dogbone tool around the edge. Indent for the main vein on soft foam.

2 For the darker variety, allow the leaf to dry and then paint the top side only with Burgundy droplet colour and gum arabic solution. Immediately remove the colour from the main vein using a cocktail stick or colour shaper. For the green variety, paint the top side

of the leaf only with Fern droplet colour and gum arabic solution.

3 Paint both leaf colours with a confectioner's glaze on the top side only to finish.

4 Tape the leaves onto a 24-gauge wire with half-width dark brown tape. Arrange them in pairs, with each pair at right angles to the previous pair.

IVY
There are several different types of ivy, with many variations on each. One of the most popular shapes is provided on page 126.

1 Make the leaves from pale green flowerpaste. When dry, dust with Autumn Green powder, followed by Aubergine.

2 Boil a kettle and pass the leaves through the steam a couple of times, until a slight sheen is achieved. Remove the colour with a cocktail stick to show the veins.

3 Fix the leaves alternately to the main stem, bending the individual stems so that each leaf is raised slightly above the main stem.

Eucalyptus

Pittosporum

RIBBON GRASSES (see pages 79, 105 and 109)
These grasses made from ribbon are invaluable for filling gaps in naturalistic flower arrangements.

1 Cut one 8cm (3in) length each of 2.5mm (⅛in) wide ribbon in cream, willow green and pine, and place a 5cm (2in) length of 30-gauge wire across the middle of all the ribbon pieces. Pull the wire down underneath and twist to secure.

2 Bind some full-width florist's tape around the base of the ribbons and wire and then cut down through them, thereby halving each one. Cut the ends of each ribbon at an angle.

DRIED GRASSES
These grasses are very useful for adding to mixed groups of flowers.

1 Cut some beige florist's tape into very narrow, pointed strips about 1cm (½in) long. Place these on hard foam and pull through under the point of a leaf aid tool. This will both stiffen and stretch the pieces slightly.

2 Bind one strip onto the end of a length of 30-gauge white wire with half-width tape, then bind down the rest of the wire. Attach the remaining pieces at intervals down the stem, taping in just enough of each piece to attach it to the wire.

TWIGS
Many leaves, such as pittosporum, broom and ivy, need to be presented on a twig. These groups of leaves are useful in the shaping of a spray.

1 There will probably be a growing point (this depends on the time of year), which can be made from either beige or nile green florist's tape. Cut a 2cm (¾in) length of half-width tape and roll half of it to a point. Bend this over until there is just a tiny lump sticking up.

2 Bind the part of the tape that has not been twisted onto a 24-gauge green wire, then cover the wire from just under this point with half-width beige, wine or dark brown tape.

3 If you want to add bulk to a twig or stem, bind on a pipe cleaner with full-width tape. You can achieve a shiny surface on a twig by rubbing it well with a leaf aid tool or the back of a dogbone tool. For the effect of growth rings, wind fine rose wire several times around the thick stem, then cover well with full-width tape.

ANEMONE LEAVES (see page 15)
1 Allow three leaves for each flower and bud. Make them with 28-gauge green wires. Cut out the shape using the No. 37 cutter. Remove surplus paste, then roll over a few of the 'fingers' with the pointed end of a cocktail stick and cut out irregular V shapes using a craft knife. Make sure the ends are as pointed as possible. Continue around the leaf, dealing with one section at a time, until it is completed.

2 Remove the leaf from the board with a palette knife, then curve the middle of the leaf on soft foam with a dogbone tool and twist the edges with your fingers. Allow to dry. Paint

with Fern droplet colour and gum arabic solution, perhaps dusting the edges with Copper dusting powder.

DAFFODIL LEAVES (see page 31)
1 Make these leaves with 28-gauge green wires, cutting out the shapes freehand (see page 126). Daffodils usually produce lots of leaves, some fairly straight and others nicely curved. Give the ends a slight twist.

2 When dry, dust with Eucalyptus powder, and the ends of the leaves with cream powder.

GERBERA LEAVES (see page 41)
1 Make the leaves with 26-gauge green wires, and in a variety of sizes. Cut an irregular shape freehand (see page 126) from green flowerpaste, keeping the edges fairly undulating, with the full length slightly curved. Work on the edges from the back with a leaf aid tool.

2 When dry, paint with Fern droplet colour and gum arabic solution.

PANSY LEAVES (see page 51)
1 Make the leaves with 28-gauge green wires. Cut out a number of leaves from green flowerpaste, using the No. 29 cutter or the real leaf stuck onto card.

2 When they are dry, paint the leaves with Fern droplet colour and gum arabic solution, immediately removing the paint from the main veins with the sharp end of a cocktail stick or a colour shaper. Cover the wire with half-width nile green florist's tape to complete.

Alchemilla

Commonly known as lady's mantle, this plant has wonderful pleated leaves, perfect for both formal and natural arrangements. The leaves have a habit of retaining droplets of water for quite some time after a shower of rain. It was these that the alchemists liked to gather to help them in their quest to make gold!

YOU WILL NEED

Cutter Nos 11 and 12

White flowerpaste (gum paste) coloured with Christmas Green paste food colour

28-gauge green wire for small leaves, 24-gauge for large leaves

Nile green florist's tape

Forest Green, Euphorbia and Snowflake dusting powders

Paint Aid

Gelatine droplets (see page 11)

Soft foam

1 (For full instructions on making and colouring leaves, see pages 62–5.) Prepare the flowerpaste (gum paste), making sure that you have plenty for the larger leaves, and cut out the leaves using the Nos 11 and 12 cutters. The edges of the larger leaves can be toothed (see page 64), while the smaller size can be treated with a serrator.

2 Lift the leaf onto some soft foam and indent in between the curves with a palette knife or leaf aid tool. Turn the leaf over (this will now be the upper surface) and indent again through the centre of the scallop

shapes. Shape the leaf with your fingers, possibly bringing forward the portion of leaf on either side of the wire.

3 When the leaves are dry, dust near the centre with a little Forest Green dusting powder, and then overall with Euphorbia. Wet a paintbrush with Paint Aid and then pick up a little Snowflake dusting powder to create a thick paste. Paint this onto the edge of the leaf very delicately.

4 Using tweezers, dip gelatine droplets in egg white and place on the leaves to look like dew.

On small leaves, use a serrator to produce a fine-toothed edge.

Indent the leaf deeply through the scallop centres using a leaf aid tool.

Paint on the white edging carefully, to emphasize the shape.

Rusty-back fern

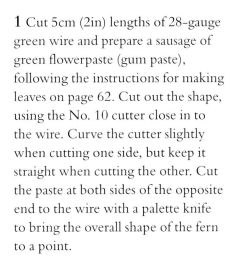

YOU WILL NEED

Cutter No. 10

Flowerpaste (gum paste) coloured with
    Christmas Green paste food colour

28-gauge green wire

30-gauge white wire

Rust and very pale cream dusting
    powders

Fern droplet colour

Gum arabic solution

Soft foam

Additional greenery helps to enhance the colour and vibrancy of the flowers in an arrangement. Ferns, especially, give an impression of depth as well as interesting form. They can be grouped or used singly.

1 Cut 5cm (2in) lengths of 28-gauge green wire and prepare a sausage of green flowerpaste (gum paste), following the instructions for making leaves on page 62. Cut out the shape, using the No. 10 cutter close in to the wire. Curve the cutter slightly when cutting one side, but keep it straight when cutting the other. Cut the paste at both sides of the opposite end to the wire with a palette knife to bring the overall shape of the fern to a point.

2 Roll each lobe with a blunt cocktail stick to change the points to rounded shapes. Turn the paste over.

3 Place the fern on soft foam and indent the main vein. If the fern will not stay upright in the correct shape, hang it from the side of a piece of polystyrene over the edge of a table.

4 When dry, dust the back with Rust powder and then paint the top surface with Fern droplet colour and gum arabic solution.

5 With smaller or younger ferns, made on 30-gauge white wires, curve the top section forwards. These young ferns have a lighter colour on the back, so dust with very pale cream powder.

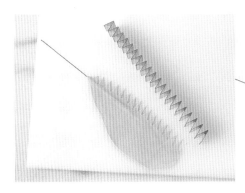

Cut out the fern shape from green paste, using the cutter close to the wire.

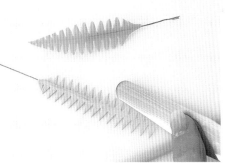

Cut the opposite end to the wire with a palette knife to create a pointed shape.

Roll the lobes with a cocktail stick to change the points to a rounded shape.

Presentation and arranging

For years cake decorators have been faced with the daunting task of incorporating their sugar flowers into arrangements, the shape of which has been dictated mainly by florists' ideas and conventions.

This approach does not, however, take into account the fact that the medium – flowerpaste (gum paste) – is quite stiff in character, and I believe we have to compensate for this stiffness by adding plenty of movement to the work. By taking a more natural approach, we can achieve much more successful results in the final presentation of our sugar flowers.

MAKING ARRANGEMENTS

You do not need to acquire the skills of a clever florist in order to present your flowers to good effect on a cake. There are other alternatives, which can be a huge help to those who are less experienced.

Mini spots, 'pepperpots' and flower picks have enabled us for the first time really to enjoy making the best of sugar flowers, without the many constraints to which florists are subject with their fresh flowers in case they wilt or petals fall. With these new aids to arranging, all you have to do is push in the wires of the flowers and leaves, and in a very

short time you will have created an attractive arrangement. Should any breakages occur, pull out the broken one and insert a new complete item. If you want part of the arrangement draped over the edge of the cake, you can simply tape several items together into a loose, semi-formal group before adding this to the rest of the arrangement.

It is a good idea to lay out the leaves and flowers on the table, or stick them into polystyrene, to give a rough idea of the overall shape and balance of colour before you carry out the final work. To make things easier and save time, cut down on the number of flowers, as these are more complex to make, and increase the amount of foliage.

All the arrangements are done away from the cake. On completion, you will then have the confidence to fix the whole arrangement directly onto the cake by inserting the flowerpick or perspex disc into the prepared hole or recess.

Be adventurous, try out the new ideas demonstrated by the cakes in

this book – and you will find the whole process a lot easier and your finished results much more pleasing.

EQUIPMENT
PERSPEX DISC
These discs are used as a ready-made base onto which a pepperpot or mini spots (see below) can be fixed.

When the cake has been covered, decide on the position of the arrangement and cut out a piece of the sugarpaste (rolled fondant) the same size as the disc, down to the marzipan. Roll and cut out a very thin layer of sugarpaste the same size as the disc and put it back in the shallow recess. When the arrangement is ready, simply manoeuvre it into place in the recess – it does not need to be stuck down. To lift the arrangement, steady it with one hand while balancing it on a palette knife and then slide it gently into place.

MINI SPOTS
Mini spots, a commercially prepared product with similar characteristics

to oasis, can be stuck onto a small silver board or, as in this book, a perspex disc. Use superglue for strength – it is safe to do so, as the glue will not be anywhere near the cake.

You will need at least three mini spots for a natural group of flowers and leaves. Push leftover white flowerpaste down in between the mini spots and then cover over all three with some more leftover white paste, then finally cover everything right up to the edge of the disc with the same covering as used on the cake, if suitable. In this book, sugarpaste is used throughout. You can then stipple on colours such as green and brown (using dilute Fern and Bamboo droplet colours) with a damp natural sponge. Do not take the colours up to the edge, but let them fade away gradually. Now push in the prepared flowers and leaves.

Wisteria is made in the same way as broom (see page 18). Use pale blue flowerpaste and dust with mauve shades.

PERSPEX 'PEPPERPOT'
This item has seven holes – one in the middle and six around the edge – so that groups of wires can be pushed in, using it like a vase. Tape several different items together at the point at which they are inserted to make one thicker stalk, which is easier to push into the hole than several finer wires. This will also help to make the arrangement more stable.

PERSPEX RULER
For arrangements on the board at the side of the cake, you can stick a mini spot or spraymaker (more suitable for one or two large flowers) onto a ruler-shaped piece of perspex. Then push the 'ruler' in under the cake as far as it will go.

FLOWER PICK
This comes in two pieces: the stand and the flower holder (see below). Fill the flower holder with leftover white flowerpaste and push in the wires of a formal or semi-formal arrangement. As with a pepperpot, you can tape several items together to make one thicker stem.

EQUIPMENT

1 Flower holder
2 Flower stand
3 Flower holder and stand
  assembled (flower pick)
4 Perspex disc plus mini spot
5 Perspex ruler
6 Spraymaker
7 Perspex ruler plus
  mini spot
8 Perspex disc plus pepperpot

A simple group of anemones and leaves arranged in a pepperpot sits neatly in a recess on the cake.

Make a hole in the cake with an empty flower pick first, as this makes it much easier to insert the final arrangement. Only use a product that is made from food-approved plastic, as this cannot be cut if an electric knife is used on the cake.

When the cake is to be cut, remove the flower arrangement and holder and place in the stand.

CRESCENT-SHAPED ARRANGEMENT
This is a relatively easy way of presenting a formal arrangement (see pages 76–9).

1 You will need two 24-gauge wires for each arm of the spray. For a 20cm (8in) cake, these should be about 15cm (6in) long. Start taping one wire with florist's tape and when you have covered about 2.5cm (1in) join in the other wire. Repeat for the other side of the spray.

2 Form a 5cm (2in) length of 28-gauge wire into a loop and twist underneath. Bend the loop at right angles to the twisted wire (A).

3 Start making one side of the spray with very small items, adding larger items as you progress, taping them to the covered wires with half-width tape. Leave plenty of space in between and use lots of leaves – they are not only essential to the overall colour and harmony of the spray, but are also easily arranged at different levels. Finish taping items onto the wires about 2.5cm (1in) from the middle of the complete shape. Bend the covered wires at right angles to the spray (B). Place this down carefully and then make a similar spray for the other half.

4 Join the two sections together with full-width tape and a little fine rose wire for extra stability. Join in the little looped wire on the inside of the curve, so that the loop stands out at the back (C). (You could bring a third arm into this arrangement if you need some height for, say, the top tier of a wedding cake.)

5 Now tape in some larger leaves and bring some forward, some back. Add the focal point, then generally fill in as necessary to complete, taping the wires underneath as you go. Trim off the wires to neaten. Finish with some more rose wire to secure and make sure it is well covered with tape, as it can be very painful if the wire sticks in your fingers while you are working.

6 Finally, stand back to view the arrangement, tweaking with tweezers where necessary (D).

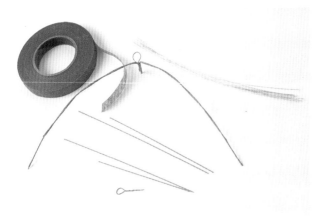

A To make a crescent-shaped formal arrangement, you will need 24-gauge wires for the two 'arms', 28-gauge wire for the loop, rose wire for strengthening, and florist's tape.

B Tape the flowers and leaves onto one 'arm' of the arrangement, leaving plenty of space between items and using a good number of leaves, then bend the wire in a gentle curve.

PRESENTING THE CAKE

Cover the cake board with sugarpaste at least two days in advance of the cake, to allow the covering to become hard.

Cover the cake at least one day ahead of marking on any side design with a craft knife or scriber, to allow the covering to harden a little. Mark any necessary measurements on the side surface before working an edging, such as a snail's trail, around the base. See also the side design templates on page 126, which will fit any shape or size of cake.

PIPING

Make piping bags more secure with a piece of half-width masking tape long enough to wrap all the way around the bag and stick to itself.

To match piping to the cake, take a piece of the sugarpaste used to cover the cake and mash it down with a little water in a bowl until it looks like thick royal icing. Use this to pipe the 'snail's trail' around the base of the cake – it will be a perfect match.

Alternatively, use royal icing matched to the cake covering, but remember when adding colour that the icing will dry fractionally lighter.

PRESSURE-PIPED RUNOUTS AND BRUSH EMBROIDERY

Pressure piping – normal piping with more pressure applied – is used for 'runouts' where a build-up of icing is required to fill a shape. In brush embroidery, royal icing is pressure-piped around the edge of a template shape and then brushed down to cover it using a damp paintbrush.

1 Cut out a piece of roasting bag to fit a wall tile and fix it in place on the tile with masking tape, making sure that the covering is really taut.

2 Cut out a strip of greaseproof paper slightly longer than the width of the tile and a little deeper than the design to be copied. Trace out the design on one end of the strip and then push this under the roasting bag. Work the design in pressure

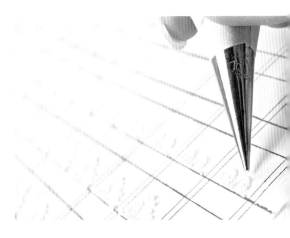

Use a roasting bag on top of the grid and pipe onto this. Keep the design of the lace simple.

piping or brush embroidery, then pull out the greaseproof strip until it is well clear of the first design and repeat the work as many times as you need. It is always wise to work a few extra pieces in case of breakages.

3 When piping 'lace', wherever possible keep to the same design throughout, as for the cakes in this book – you will work much more quickly if you know the pattern well.

C When both 'arms' have been completed, join them together using full-width florist's tape and a little rose wire for extra strength. Join in the looped wire inside the curve.

D Add in larger leaves and the focal point, then fill in as required to complete the arrangement. Stand back to view the overall effect, adjusting with tweezers as necessary.

cakes

English garden

The open rose is so delightfully English, growing wild in hedgerows in early summer, while the little dianthus, or pink, is a lovely reminder of old-fashioned cottage gardens. I have chosen pink, white and green as the colours to reflect the freshness at the onset of summer, and these flowers and their many leaves are just right for this idea.

CAKE AND DECORATION
20cm (8in) oval cake and 33cm (13in) oval board covered in champagne ivory sugarpaste (rolled fondant)
Matching royal icing
Leftover white flowerpaste (gum paste)
Pink, Euphorbia and yellow dusting powders
106cm (42in) matching velvet ribbon, 1.5cm (⅝in) wide
Double-sided adhesive tape

SPECIAL EQUIPMENT
Flower pick
Perspex disc with 3 mini spots
No. 0 piping tube (tip)
Lace, rose and calyx templates (see page 126)
Wall tile
Roasting bag
Masking tape
Greaseproof paper

FLOWERS FOR THE TOP ARRANGEMENT
Spray of open roses and leaves (see pages 48–9)

FLOWERS FOR THE BASE ARRANGEMENT
Dianthus (see pages 34–5)
Ribbon grasses (see page 67)

1 Make a hole in the top of the cake, slightly off centre, ready to take the flower pick. Push a perspex disc partway under the cake where you want the flower arrangement to be positioned, and then stick on three mini spots (A). Measure and mark the height for the lace around the side of the cake and the

positions for the eight rose designs, then pipe a snail's trail of matching sugarpaste (rolled fondant) all the way around the base of the cake using a No. 0 piping tube (tip).

2 Make up the flowers and leaves for the top of the cake, as this will give you ideas for the arrangement, then make up the crescent-shaped spray following the instructions on pages 72–3. Put some leftover white flowerpaste (gum paste) in the flower pick and push in the completed spray. Insert the pick and spray into the prepared hole in the top of the cake.

3 Using the lace template, pipe a total of at least 25 pieces of lace in matching royal icing, using a No. 0 piping tube (see page 78) (B).

THE TOP ARRANGEMENT (SEE PAGES 72–3)
You will need at least ten open roses, a few buds and 14 sets of leaves for this arrangement, but the exact number is your own choice.

4 For the rose and calyx design on the side of the cake, make some fairly soft royal icing and colour it with pink dusting powder for the rose, Euphorbia for the calyx and yellow for the stamens.

Pressure-pipe eight roses and eight calyces, plus a few extra pieces in case of breakages – piping the roses and calyces separately makes them easier to handle (C). When working the roses, pipe the

A Push the perspex disc and mini spots partway under the cake in the required position on the board. Dianthus flowers and leaves and ribbon grasses will be arranged in this later.

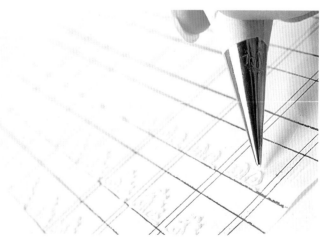

B Pipe at least 25 repetitions of the lace design in royal icing, following the template. Leave the icing to dry completely before removing the shapes from the tile.

C To work repetitions of the rose and calyx designs, pull the strip of greaseproof paper on which the outlines are drawn along under the roasting bag and pipe the next design.

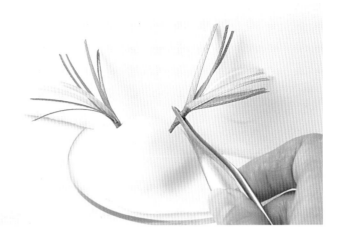

D Using tweezers, push ribbon grasses into the mini spots on the disc to begin building up the side arrangement. Then add dianthus flowers and leaves, and fill any gaps with more grasses.

back petals first, followed by the front. Flood icing into both shapes and dry under a lamp. When dry, pipe little yellow dots into the centre of each rose.

5 When completely dry, remove the shapes from the tile. To fix the lace, roses and calyces in place, pipe on about seven dots of royal icing with a No. 0 piping tube and then push in a piece of lace on top. Fix on two more pieces in the same way, then pipe on large dots of icing and fix on the calyx first, slightly overlapped by the rose. There should be three pieces of lace between roses.

6 For the base arrangement, cover the mini spots with leftover flowerpaste (see page 71). Paint with egg white, cover with a layer of champagne ivory sugarpaste and trim off near the edge of

the disc. Push in the ribbon grasses, then the dianthus flowers, and fill any spaces with more grasses (D).

7 To complete, stick the velvet ribbon around the edge of the cake board with double-sided adhesive tape.

THE BASE ARRANGEMENT
This is made up from a selection of dianthus flowers in different shades of pink and white, plenty of grey-green dianthus foliage, and as many ribbon grasses as you like to fill in any gaps.

Iris mosaic

I don't know if the world loved irises before Monet and the other Impressionists found them, but the blooms are always show-stoppers. Wonderful shapes are to be found among the leaves, and there is an amazing colour range in the flowers. To copy them life-size could be difficult, hence the small impression of a large flower that I have used.

CAKE AND DECORATION
20cm (8in) oval cake and
   33cm (13in) oval board,
   covered in champagne
   ivory sugarpaste (rolled
   fondant)
Matching royal icing
Leftover white flowerpaste
   (gum paste)
Droplet colours of your
   choice, for mosaic pattern
Bamboo and Fern droplet
   colours
106cm (42in) matching velvet
   ribbon, 1.5cm (⅝in) wide
Double-sided adhesive tape

SPECIAL EQUIPMENT
Perspex disc with
   3 mini spots
Perspex disc with 1 mini spot
No. 0 piping tube (tip)
Mosaic cutter
Natural sponge

**FLOWERS FOR THE
   TOP AND BASE
   ARRANGEMENTS**
Iris flowers and leaves (see
   pages 42–3)
Ribbon grasses (see page 67)
Filler foliage

1 Cut a recess in the sugarpaste (rolled fondant) on the top of the cake, the size of the perspex disc. Fix three mini spots to the disc for the top arrangement, and one to the disc for the base arrangement. Cover the disc for the top with matching sugarpaste. Push the disc for the side in under the cake until it is correctly

positioned. Pipe dots of matching royal icing around the top recess using a No. 0 piping tube (tip).

2 Draw an iris pattern on the board with a pencil, simplifying the flower and leaf shapes (A), or make up a different pattern but still using the colours of the flower arrangement. Using the mosaic cutter (B), cut out plenty of small mosaic pieces from white flowerpaste (gum paste) coloured with bamboo droplet colour to match the cake covering. To work out how many you need, cut out and place enough pieces to cover a 5cm (2in) square, then multiply up to fit around the board. The number of coloured pieces required depends on the pattern. Make about 20 in each colour to start with, and then extras if you need them.

THE TOP ARRANGEMENT
For an arrangement like this, I usually work with odd numbers of flowers, so three in any one colour is a good place to start. Make many more leaves than flowers – there will be plenty of room for them to be positioned at various angles.

3 The mosaic pieces are easier to use if they are hard enough to hold with tweezers. Pipe royal icing onto the back of each mosaic piece and then position it on the board. Complete the pattern first (C), then fill in the ivory pieces. Try to follow the line of the edge of the board, working inwards in rows (D). You may need to cut some irregular pieces to fit in small spaces. If you have to cut any awkward shapes you need not wait for them to dry – just cut to fit, pipe icing

A Draw out the mosaic design on the cake board. You can use an iris design, or choose something completely different but still using the colours of the flower arrangement.

B Use a special mosaic cutter to cut out small pieces of coloured flowerpaste for your design. Leave to dry until they are hard enough to be picked up with tweezers.

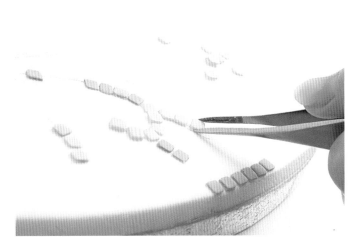

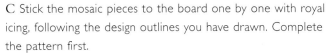

C Stick the mosaic pieces to the board one by one with royal icing, following the design outlines you have drawn. Complete the pattern first.

D When filling in the ivory-coloured background, follow the line of the edge of the cake board, working your way carefully inwards in rows.

onto the board and put in place. Do not try a very complicated design unless you have plenty of patience!

4 Add a row of ivory mosaic around the base of the cake, rather than piping a snail's trail. These pieces are more difficult to put on than those in the flat design: it is better to put the royal icing on the back of the pieces than on the board (otherwise it tends to ooze out from underneath).

5 With a damp sponge, stipple some diluted Bamboo and Fern droplet colour onto the paste on the disc and put in the iris flowers, leaves and ribbon grasses. If you have any spare leaves of a different shape, push these in at the front. For the base arrangement, cover the mini spot with leftover white flowerpaste and put

in a much smaller group of iris flowers, leaves and ribbon grasses.

6 Fix some green mosaic pieces around the top recess, then slip the disc and flowers into place. To complete, stick the velvet ribbon to the edge of the cake board with double-sided adhesive tape.

THE BOARD DESIGN

The iris pattern for the mosaic on the cake board is a stylized version of the flower arrangements on top of the cake and on the board. Keep the design simple unless you have endless patience!

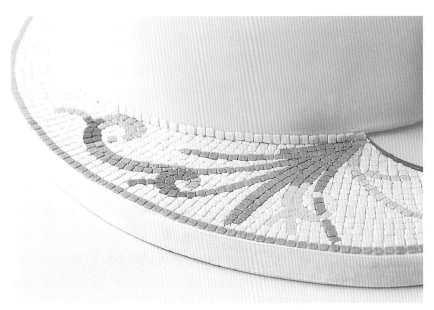

Special celebration

With this cake for a special occasion, I have combined some of the lemon-yellow and mauve flowers with which we are all familiar from florists' bouquets and sprays. Care needs to be taken when arranging them, but it is not essential to put in so many items: I decided to mass the flowers, as I wanted to keep the cake design itself to a minimum.

CAKE AND DECORATION

20cm (8in) square cake and 33cm (13in) square board, covered in champagne ivory sugarpaste (rolled fondant)

Matching royal icing

Florist's tape

134cm (53in) matching velvet ribbon, 1.5cm (⅝in) wide

Double-sided adhesive tape

SPECIAL EQUIPMENT

Perspex disc with pepperpot

No. 0 piping tube (tip)

Side design and lace templates (see page 126)

Wall tile

Roasting bag

Masking tape

Greaseproof paper

FLOWERS FOR THE TOP ARRANGEMENT

Eustoma (see pages 36–7)

Pittosporum leaves (see page 66)

Carnations (see pages 20–21)

Freesias (see pages 38–9)

Roses (see pages 52–3)

Aucuba leaves (see page 65)

Gerberas (see pages 40–41)

1 Cut a recess in the sugarpaste (rolled fondant) in the middle of the top of the cake, the size of the perspex disc. Roll out and cut a very thin layer of matching sugarpaste and lay it back in the recess. Pipe dots of matching royal icing around this circle with a No. 0 piping tube (tip).

2 Using the large and small side design templates, for the sides and corners of the cake respectively, mark the position for the lace. Pipe a snail's trail of matching sugarpaste around the base of the cake using a No. 0 piping tube. Using the lace template, pipe about 70 pieces in matching royal icing (see page 73). Following the marked curves, pipe about seven dots of icing at a time and push in a piece of lace on top. Repeat all the way around the cake to make a continuous band of lace (A).

3 There are plenty of flowers in this arrangement, so you will need to plan it out fairly carefully – perhaps by taping some of the items together and pushing them into a polystyrene block in the general shape of the arrangement, but with plenty of space between them to

THE TOP ARRANGEMENT
A wide selection of flowers and foliage is used for this design. When preparing the freesias, make up three extra sprays of buds to be used separately around the arrangement.

avoid breakages. Look at the height and spread of the whole arrangement at this stage, and trim accordingly. It may be that some flowers need to be taller or shorter so that you can get everything in without the heads being in danger of knocking against each other.

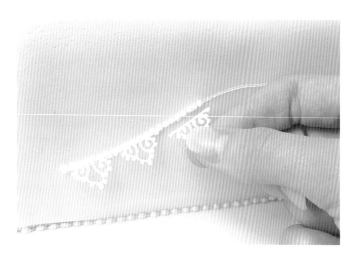

A Pipe on dots of royal icing and then gently push in the lace, keeping the angle uniform as you work. You will need about 70 pieces of lace to complete the design.

B Arrange the flowers and leaves in the pepperpot and then slip the arrangement very carefully into the prepared recess in the top of the cake.

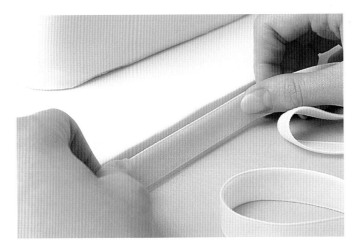

C Stick double-sided adhesive tape all the way round the edge of the board (it will not stick to the sugarpaste), then fix on the velvet ribbon, starting from the back.

D Once everything is in position, stand back and look at the flower arrangement, then use tweezers to make any final adjustments that may be necessary.

4 Make the eustoma the central focal point of the arrangement and cluster pittosporum leaves and carnations around it. You may need to strip down each stem to one wire at the base, so that when taped together they will fit into the centre hole of the pepperpot. Push in the group stem securely: any space and the flowers could swing around.

5 Now make the rest of the flowers in two separate groups – freesias, roses and aucuba leaves; then gerberas and freesia buds – to alternate around the arrangement. Give the freesias, roses and aucuba leaves a length of wire about the same as the height of the middle of the arrangement or longer, so that they add breadth to the display. Turn down the last 2cm (¾in) of each wire to push into the pepperpot.

6 Slip the flower arrangement and disc into place in the recess (B). Stick the velvet ribbon around the edge of the cake board with double-sided adhesive tape (C). Finally, stand back and look at the arrangement, tweaking with tweezers where necessary (D).

THE SIDE DESIGN
The repeated lace pattern, piped in royal icing, is attached to the cake following the lines of the curved side templates. The overall effect is both simple and pretty.

Winter colour

I wanted to design a cake that would introduce some sparkle and vivid colours to any winter event. When I made the leaves for the anemone they reminded me of the 'Jack Frost fingers' we used to see on windows before the advent of central heating, especially around Christmas time.

CAKE AND DECORATION

20cm (8in) square cake and 33cm (13in) square board, covered in champagne ivory sugarpaste (rolled fondant)

Matching royal icing

White flowerpaste (gum paste)

Gelatine droplets (see page 11)

White Hologram dusting powder

Gum arabic solution

134cm (53in) matching velvet ribbon, 1.5cm (⅝in) wide

Double-sided adhesive tape

SPECIAL EQUIPMENT

Perspex disc and pepperpot

No. 0 piping tube (tip)

Cutter Nos 1 and 37

Soft foam

Ripple foam

FLOWERS FOR THE TOP ARRANGEMENT

Anemone flowers and leaves (see pages 14–15 and 67)

1 Cut a recess in the sugarpaste (rolled fondant) in the middle of the top of the cake, the size of the perspex disc. Roll and cut out a very thin layer of matching sugarpaste and lay this back in the recess. Pipe dots of matching royal icing around this circle using a No. 0 piping tube (tip). Measure and mark a straight line around the sides of the cake about 6cm (2½in) up from the board. Pipe dots of

icing along this line, then pipe a snail's trail of matching sugarpaste around the base of the cake.

2 Cut out several leaf shapes from white flowerpaste (gum paste) using the No. 37 cutter. Follow the instructions given for making anemone leaves on page 67, cutting out all the V shapes. On soft foam, curve the bottom of the leaf using a dogbone tool. Turn the leaf over and curve the 'fingers' backwards using a leaf aid tool: start at the points and pull the tool gently but firmly over the paste, which should then curl. The hook at the other end of the tool should remain upright – if it tends to turn over you are probably applying too much pressure, and the paste will not curl so well. Allow the leaf to stiffen slightly, supported in ripple foam (A).

THE TOP ARRANGEMENT
The number of flowers you use is your choice, but try to include a selection of the colour range. Keep to an uneven number, and include some buds as well.

3 When you have made three or four leaves, stick them onto the cake directly below the line of piped dots using royal icing (B), keeping them at the same angle.

4 When you have made and stuck leaves all the way around the cake (you will

need about 32), attach gelatine droplets to the leaves wherever you can reach without risk of breakages. Dip a gelatine droplet in egg white and then in White Hologram dusting powder, pipe a dot of royal icing onto the leaf and push in the droplet, so that it sticks out slightly (C).

A Curve the 'fingers' of the anemone leaves using a leaf aid tool, then leave the shapes to stiffen, supporting them on ripple foam.

B Make several leaves at a time, then pipe a large dot of royal onto the cake directly below the piped line of smaller dots and fix the leaf to this.

C Pipe a dot of royal icing onto the leaf shape, dip a gelatine droplet in egg white and then in White Hologram dusting powder, and fix to the leaf so that it sticks out slightly.

D Paint the little flowerpaste star shapes with gum arabic solution and then brush each one with White Hologram dusting powder, before fixing to the cake with royal icing.

5 Cut out the same number of stars as leaves from white flowerpaste using the No. 1 cutter. When dry, paint with gum arabic solution and then brush with White Hologram dusting powder (D). Fix a star to the cake above each leaf using dots of royal icing.

6 Decide on the height of the flowers and then tape in an extra leaf just above where the stem will sit in the pepperpot. Add some extra foliage if liked, taping it to the anemone stems. Start putting in flowers from the centre, keeping everything as upright as possible so that you can push in the lower items without risk of breakages. On the outside pieces, bend the last 2cm (³⁄₄in) or so of the stem almost at right angles so that you can push them in more easily without knocking the centre flowers and leaves.

Slip the flower arrangement and disc into place in the recess. Once in position, adjust the flower stems and angles, mainly pulling them downwards.

7 To complete, stick the matching velvet ribbon to the edge of the cake board with double-sided adhesive tape.

THE SIDE DESIGN
The shape of the anemone leaves in the flower arrangement is echoed here in this pretty design around the sides of the cake. You will need around 32 leaves and stars in total.

Springtime in Wales

I first started demonstrating the art of making sugar flowers in Wales, so with this in mind I decided to use the Welsh emblem of the daffodil as the main feature for this pretty cake, noting from a design viewpoint that the stalks and leaves play a big part in enhancing the flowers. I kept the side pattern to a minimum so that the design remains simple.

CAKE AND DECORATION

20cm (8in) oval cake and 33cm (13in) oval board, covered in champagne ivory sugarpaste (rolled fondant)

Matching royal icing

Leftover white flowerpaste (gum paste)

Pale green flowerpaste

Fern and Bamboo droplet colours

Gum arabic solution

Small daffodil heads (see pages 30–31)

106cm (42in) matching velvet ribbon, 1.5cm (⅝in) wide

Double-sided adhesive tape

SPECIAL EQUIPMENT

No. 0 piping tube (tip)

Perspex disc with 3 mini spots

Perspex ruler with 1 mini spot

Side design templates (see page 126)

1 Cut a recess in the sugarpaste (rolled fondant) on top of the cake, the size of the perspex disc. Pipe dots of matching royal icing around this using a No. 0 piping tube (tip). Fix three mini spots to the disc for the top and one to the perspex ruler, then slide this under the cake in the correct

position, as far as it will go. The weight of the cake will keep it in place. Cover the three mini spots on the disc with leftover white flowerpaste (gum paste).

2 Mark the position of the side design lightly using a scriber or similar tool. Roll out some pale green flowerpaste and, using the side design templates, cut out two large sizes and one small (A). Keeping two pieces under cover, start to shape the other one. Cut out narrow V shapes of varying depths all along the curved edge. Using a leaf aid tool, mark indentations to represent the leaves and stems (B). Turn the shape over, paint on some egg white or water, then press the shape gently onto the side of the cake so that it sticks all the way along. Work and fix the other two shapes in the same way.

THE TOP ARRANGEMENT

The size and colours of the daffodils can vary, as can the height and angle at which the flowers are set into the arrangement. Plenty of leaves and several different kinds of foliage help to enhance the fresh colours of the blooms.

FLOWERS FOR THE TOP ARRANGEMENT

Daffodil flowers and leaves (see pages 30–31 and 67)
Alchemilla leaves (see page 68)
Ivy leaves (see page 66)
Rusty-back fern leaves (see page 69)
Filler foliage

FLOWERS FOR THE BASE ARRANGEMENT

Daffodil flowers and leaves
Ivy leaves
Rusty-back fern leaves
Filler foliage

3 Using Fern droplet colour and gum arabic solution, paint some sections as leaves and stalks, leaving the remaining sections the original green to create a feeling of light coming through the leaves (C). Pipe a snail's trail of matching sugarpaste around the base of the cake using the No. 0 piping tube. You may

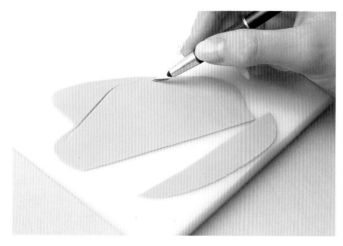

A Use the side design templates to cut out one small and two large shapes from pale green flowerpaste. After shaping and painting, these will form the leaves for the little daffodils.

B Use a leaf aid tool to mark a series of indentations along each shape, to represent the long, narrow leaves and flower stems of the daffodils.

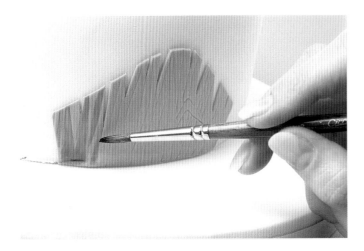

C Paint some sections with Fern droplet colour and gum arabic solution, leaving the remaining sections the original green colour to give a feeling of light filtering through the leaves.

D Make the daffodil flowers for the side decoration using the smaller petal shapes and make the little trumpets separately. Fix these in place once the petals are stuck to the cake.

like to do this only between the sections of the side design (as shown).

4 Make some daffodil flowers following the instructions on pages 30–31. Work with the smaller petal shapes and make the little trumpets separately (D). Arrange the flowers in groups, some overlapping slightly, then fix the trumpets in place with a small amount of royal icing.

5 Arrange the main group of flowers and leaves in the mini spots, then slip the flower arrangement and disc into the recess in the top of the cake.

6 Cover the mini spot for the side arrangement with leftover white flowerpaste, then with sugarpaste, and stipple some diluted Bamboo and Fern droplet colour over the middle of the

domed area. Cut the paste in gentle curves. Arrange the flowers and leaves in the mini spot.

7 To complete, stick the matching velvet ribbon to the edge of the cake board with double-sided adhesive tape.

THE SIDE DESIGN
You will need about 25 small daffodil heads to complete the design around the side of the cake. These are fixed among the 'leaves', at different heights and sometimes overlapping.

Summer harmony

The scabious is a very delicate flower that is not difficult to make, but is tremendously effective in giving the feeling of peaceful, sunny summer days. As I had used the same cutter for both the scabious and the broom, I thought it would be appropriate to use the shape again as a feature on the side of the cake.

CAKE AND DECORATION

20cm (8in) round cake and 33cm (13in) round board, covered in champagne ivory sugarpaste (rolled fondant)

Matching royal icing

Flowerpaste (gum paste) coloured mauve as for scabious flowers (see page 55)

Platinum Lilac dusting powder

Gelatine droplets (see page 11)

Nile green florist's tape

106cm (42in) matching velvet ribbon, 1.5cm (⅝in) wide

Double-sided adhesive tape

SPECIAL EQUIPMENT

Perspex disc with pepperpot

No. 0 piping tube (tip)

Cutter No. 3

FLOWERS FOR THE TOP ARRANGEMENT

Scabious flowers and leaves (see pages 54–5)

Broom flowers and leaves (see pages 18–19)

Mock orange blossom (see pages 46–7)

Alchemilla leaves (see page 68)

1 Cut a recess in the sugarpaste (rolled fondant) in the middle of the top of the cake, to match the size of the perspex disc. Roll and cut out a very thin layer of matching ivory sugarpaste and lay this back in the recess. Pipe dots of matching royal icing around this circle using a No. 0 piping tube (tip). Measure and mark a straight line around the sides of

the cake about 5cm (2in) up from the surface of the board (A). Pipe dots of royal icing along this line, then pipe a snail's trail of matching sugarpaste around the base of the cake.

2 Roll out the mauve flowerpaste (gum paste) and dust with Platinum Lilac dusting powder (B). Cut out several shapes using the No. 3 cutter – do not try to cut out all the shapes in one go, as they will begin to dry out. Work the shapes in exactly the same way as the petals of the scabious flowers (see pages 54–5, step 2), but thin down only the three main petals, plus the sides and end of the single one. Do not fold this petal over, but bend the base forward so that when it is fixed onto the cake the three petals will come away from the side (C).

THE TOP ARRANGEMENT
The relatively large scabious flowers are complemented in this arrangement by smaller mock orange and broom, finished off with the contrasting shape of alchemilla leaves.

3 Starting from the back of the cake, pipe a small amount of royal icing on the back of the single petal and place it directly under the row of piped dots (D). Pipe another dot on either side of the

petal to secure. When there are five or six shapes still to go, judge whether you will need to push them closer together or space them further apart, so that the last one sits comfortably in place.

A Measure and mark a straight line around the sides of the cake using a craft knife or scriber. Then pipe a line of dots of matching royal icing right around the cake.

B Make up the mauve flowerpaste by mixing two separate pastes, one coloured with Royal Blue droplet colour and the other with French Pink. Dust with Platinum Lilac powder.

C Shape the petals by bending the base of the single petal forward – when it is fixed to the cake, the three other petals will come away from the side.

D Fix the petal shape to the cake directly below the row of piped dots, using royal icing. Then pipe another dot on either side of the top of the shape, to make sure it is held securely.

4 Put out a pile of gelatine droplets so you can select those that are roughly the same size. Pick up a droplet with tweezers and pipe on two dots of royal icing directly opposite each other, then use one of the dots to fix it in place, just under and touching the middle petal.

5 Work out roughly how you are going to arrange the flowers. Tape several stems together at the same point, so that when the group stalk is pushed into the pepperpot the flowers still look separate. Start inserting the flowers in the centre and work outwards. On the outside pieces, tape in alchemilla leaves, then bend the last 2cm (¾in) of the stems almost at right angles so that you can push them in without knocking the centre flowers and leaves. Fix gelatine droplets on the alchemilla leaves with

egg white to look like dew. Slip the flower arrangement into the recess.

6 To complete, stick the matching velvet ribbon to the edge of the cake board with double-sided adhesive tape.

THE SIDE DESIGN

You will need about 50 petal shapes to complete the design around the side of the cake. Once fixed in position, these are decorated uniformly with gelatine droplets.

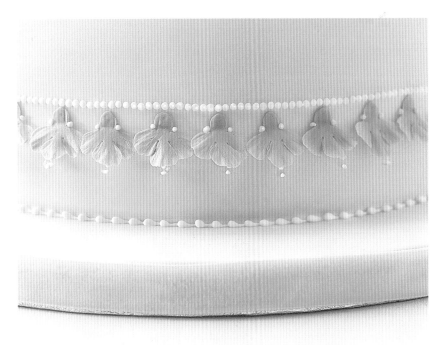

Autumn glow

The chrysanthemum is perhaps the best-known flower that offers us an opportunity to display the lovely glowing colours of autumn. I chose delicate sycamore seeds with autumnal colouring as an informal edging, with gelatine droplets added to lighten the effect. Colour is the main consideration throughout this design.

CAKE AND DECORATION

20cm (8in) round cake and 33cm (13in) round board, covered in champagne ivory sugarpaste (rolled fondant)

Matching royal icing

Flowerpaste (gum paste) coloured with Bamboo droplet colour for seeds, Christmas Green paste food colour for leaves

Copper, Mustard and Burgundy dusting powders

Gelatine droplets (see page 11)

Nile green florist's tape

106cm (42in) matching velvet ribbon, 1.5cm (⅝in) wide

Double-sided adhesive tape

SPECIAL EQUIPMENT

Perspex disc and pepperpot

No. 0 piping tube (tip)

Cutter Nos 43 and/or 14 and 15

Pins

Polystyrene tile

1 Cut a recess in the sugarpaste (rolled fondant) in the middle of the top of the cake, the size of the perspex disc. Roll and cut out a very thin layer of ivory sugarpaste and lay this back in the recess. Pipe dots of matching royal icing around this circle using a No. 0 piping tube (tip), then pipe a snail's trail around the base of the cake.

2 Cut out about eight sycamore seeds for each group from beige flowerpaste (gum paste) using cutter No. 43 and/or

by removing the middle petal from cutter Nos 14 and 15 (A). Dust the shapes with Copper, Mustard and Burgundy powders (B). Cut out ivy leaves in three different sizes from green flowerpaste and cut the edges with a knife (see page 64) to look like sycamore leaves, then dust the edges with Burgundy. Pin the seeds and leaves to a polystyrene tile (C), then hold up to a boiling kettle to steam. This will blend the colours and ensure no loose powder drops onto the board.

3 Fix the seeds to the cake with royal icing, starting at the bottom with the largest and working upwards to finish with the smallest. Do not make the arrangement too precise, and overlap the seeds in places. Then fix on the three sycamore leaves with icing, working in a curve from smallest to largest at the top.

THE TOP ARRANGEMENT
Aim to keep the flower
heads well apart, using
leaves and buds to help
with spacing. Use the
lightest-coloured flowers
 to provide the height.

**FLOWERS FOR THE TOP
ARRANGEMENT**
Chrysanthemum flowers and
    leaves (see pages 22–3)
Ivy leaves (see page 66)
Filler foliage

4 Simple designs can actually require more planning, as space can be used as a foil against very busy areas where there is a lot of display work. With this in mind, measure how much space the first group of seeds and leaves takes up, then work out how many groups are required around the cake (there are five on the cake shown) and the rough distance between them. When all the groups are

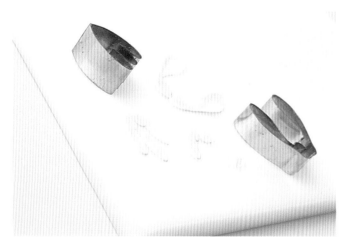

A Cut out the sycamore seeds from beige flowerpaste, using cutter Nos 43 and/or 14 and 15. Using both would allow you to make seeds in a range of sizes.

B Use three dusting powder colours – Copper, Mustard and Burgundy – to achieve the authentic autumnal shades of the sycamore seeds.

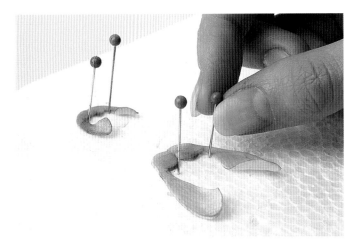

C Pin the seed and leaf shapes carefully to a polystyrene tile and then steam them with a kettle to blend the colours and ensure no loose powder drops onto the cake board.

D Using tweezers, place gelatine drops on the underside of the wings of the sycamore seeds and on the tips of the ivy leaves, fixing them in place with a drop of royal icing.

in place, pipe little dots of ivory royal icing in spiral curves between the groups of seeds and leaves, to give a better overall shape to the design.

5 Pick up a gelatine droplet with tweezers and pipe on two dots of royal icing directly opposite each other, then use one of these to fix it to the under-side of the wings of the seeds and tips of the leaves (D). Only put droplets where you can reach without risk of breakages.

6 Arrange the flowers and leaves in the pepperpot, working from the middle out. Tape a number of items together to fit in each hole of the pepperpot. I used a few wild geranium leaves (cut freehand, see page 126), dusted with Burgundy powder at the edges, as filler foliage, but any roundish leaves would

work well. Slip the arrangement and disc into place in the recess.

7 To complete, stick the matching velvet ribbon to the edge of the cake board with double-sided adhesive tape.

THE SIDE DESIGN

Each grouped arrangement of eight large and small sycamore seeds is topped by ivy leaves, their edges cut to transform them into sycamore leaves.

Scottish meadow

CAKE AND DECORATION

20cm (8in) square cake and
  35cm (14in) hexagonal
  board, covered in ivory
  sugarpaste (rolled
  fondant)
Matching royal icing,
  coloured with Empress
  Purple dusting powder
  for thistle flower, Dark
  Eucalyptus for calyx
Flowerpaste (gum paste)
  coloured with Christmas
  Green paste food colour
  plus Heraldic Black
  droplet colour for thistle
  leaves, Royal Blue dusting
  powder for edging pieces
Leftover white flowerpaste
Bamboo and Fern droplet
  colours
Gelatine droplets (see
  page 11)
134cm (53in) ivory velvet
  ribbon, 1.5cm (⅝in) wide
Double-sided adhesive tape

SPECIAL EQUIPMENT

Perspex disc with
  3 mini spots
Nos 0 and 1 piping tubes
  (tips)
Wall tile and roasting bag
Masking tape
Greaseproof paper
Thistle templates (see
  page 126)
Cutter Nos 47 and 48
Soft foam and natural sponge

As my family came originally from Scotland, I wanted to design a cake to reflect this influence but using something other than the traditional tartan theme. I set out to work the Scottish flag as a pattern around the edge of the board, but soon realized how difficult the precision work would be and so changed to a simpler geometric design.

1 Cut a recess in the sugarpaste (rolled fondant) in the top of the cake, the same size as the perspex disc. Pipe dots of matching royal icing around this circle using a No. 0 piping tube (tip). Measure and mark the height of the thistle flowers around the sides of the cake.

2 Prepare the tile and trace the thistle-head shape from the template onto a strip of greaseproof paper (see page 73).

Pressure-pipe purple royal icing across the top of the thistle shape with a No. 1 piping tube, and then with a wet paintbrush pull it down to the calyx. Fill in the calyx by pressure-piping with green royal icing, then draw the wet paintbrush across it to create a diamond pattern (A). You will need eight thistle shapes in all, plus a few extras in case of any breakages. When dry, remove from the tile.

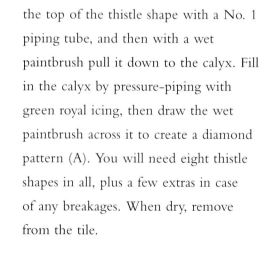

3 Cut out the thistle leaves freehand (see page 126) from pale green flowerpaste (gum paste), working on a lightly greased board (B). Start by cutting leaves about 4cm (1½in) long and gradually reduce the length as you cut out more. Using a leaf aid tool, indent each leaf heavily for the main vein. Fix five leaves on the first layer on the cake with royal icing and

THE TOP ARRANGEMENT

Keep the arrangement dome shaped, but with no rigid balance of shapes. The big alchemilla leaves take up a lot of space: overlap them and position them at different heights.

FLOWERS FOR THE TOP ARRANGEMENT

Pansy flowers and leaves (see pages 50–51 and 67)

White heather (see page 60)

Bluebell flowers and leaves (see pages 16–17)

Cornflowers and leaves (see pages 26–7)

Rusty-back fern (see page 69)

Alchemilla leaves (see page 68)

Ribbon grasses (see page 67)

Filler foliage

then hang three on the next layer, alternating these with the first (C). Put the leaves straight onto the cake as you work them, lifting the points away from the side. Support them on soft foam while you work the next few leaves. Finally, fix the thistle flower in position at the top.

A Pressure-pipe the thistle flower and calyx shapes with purple and green royal icing, then create the characteristic diamond pattern on the calyx by drawing a wet brush across the icing.

B Working on a lightly greased board, cut out the thistle leaf shapes freehand from flowerpaste coloured with Christmas Green paste food colour plus a few drops of Heraldic Black.

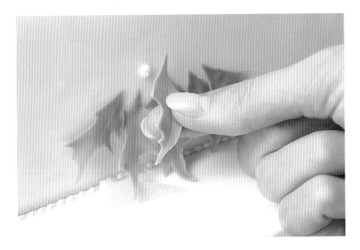

C As you add layers of leaves, alternate them with those on the previous layer. Lift the leaf points away from the side of the cake and support on soft foam while you work more leaves.

D Alternate the two triangle shapes around the edge of the board and the circle on top of the cake. Fix in place by piping dots of royal icing around each shape.

4 Using cutter Nos. 47 and 48, cut out plenty of both shapes from blue flowerpaste. Alternating the shapes, position them around the edge of the board and the circle of piped dots on top of the cake, then pipe little dots of royal icing around them to fix in place (D).

5 Fix the mini spots to the disc, then cover with leftover white flowerpaste (see page 71). Paint with egg white, cover with sugarpaste and trim. Stipple on diluted Bamboo and Fern droplet colour with a damp sponge, fading away at the edge. Push in the flowers and leaves, starting in the middle and working outwards. Add ribbon grasses to fill in any gaps. Large leaves such as alchemilla make a good foil to the busyness of the other plants. Adjust the final arrangement as necessary, then stick

gelatine droplets on the alchemilla leaves with egg white to look like dew. Slip the arrangement and disc into place.

6 To complete, stick the matching velvet ribbon to the edge of the cake board with double-sided adhesive tape.

THE SIDE DESIGN
To complete the eight thistles around the sides of the cake, you will need a total of about 96 leaf shapes in a range of sizes. Two different triangle shapes alternate around the board.

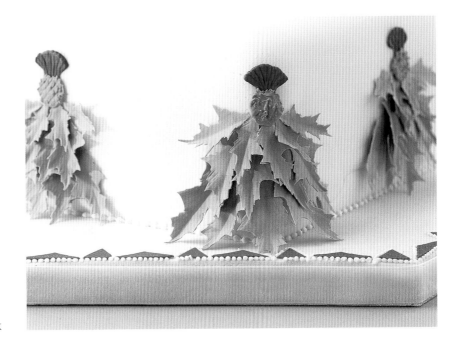

Spirit of Ireland

The beautiful scenery on Ireland's west coast gave me the idea for this cake. To add interest to the group of snowdrops, I have used a shamrock-style leaf — including, of course, a couple of four-leaved versions, essential for good luck. Everyone is familiar with the little daisy used for the side arrangement, which also suited the design well.

CAKE AND DECORATION

20cm (8in) oval cake and 33cm (13in) oval board, covered in champagne ivory sugarpaste (rolled fondant)

Matching royal icing

Flowerpaste (gum paste) coloured with Iris dusting powder for distant hills, a variety of greens plus brown and yellow for lower hills and trees (see step 3), red or orange for roofs

Heraldic Black, Bamboo and Fern droplet colours

Melon paste food colour

Leftover white flowerpaste

Oak, Mustard and White Hologram dusting powders

106cm (42in) matching velvet ribbon, 1.5cm (⅝in) wide

Double-sided adhesive tape

SPECIAL EQUIPMENT

Perspex disc with 3 mini spots

Perspex ruler with 1 mini spot

No. 0 piping tube (tip)

Cutter No. 49 and various cutters for trees (see step 4)

1 Cut a recess in the sugarpaste (rolled fondant) in the top of the cake, the size of the perspex disc. Pipe dots of matching royal icing around this using a No. 0 piping tube (tip). Fix a mini spot to the end of the perspex ruler and slide under the cake, in the correct position.

2 For the scenery, roll out some pale mauve flowerpaste (gum paste) very thinly and cut out shapes for the far

distant hills: the highest peaks should measure about 4cm (1½in) from the board. Put a little water onto the side of the cake (not above the level of the hills as it will show), then stick on the shapes — they need not be continuous (A).

3 Roll out some green flowerpaste very thinly and cut out shapes for the lower hills, working in sections. Use a selection of greens: for very dark, add Heraldic Black droplet colour; for very pale, add Melon paste food colour. You can also use light browns and yellows, but most pieces should be in green shades (B). Stick the shapes to the cake.

4 Cut out trees from flowerpaste in a range of greens (see step 3), using various cutters such as half a traditional-style carnation, small Christmas trees, part of

THE TOP ARRANGEMENT
Massed snowdrop flowers
and leaves are set off by
a single daisy flower and
scalloped shamrock leaves.

FLOWERS FOR THE TOP
ARRANGEMENT
Snowdrop flowers and
    leaves (see pages 56–7)
Shamrock leaves (see
    page 65)
Daisy flower and leaves
    (see pages 32–3)
Filler foliage

FLOWERS FOR THE BASE
ARRANGEMENT
Daisy flowers and leaves
    (see pages 32–3)
Shamrock leaves (see
    page 65)
Autumn leaves (see step 6)
Ribbon grasses (see
    page 67)

single petals, perhaps an orchid lip (C). Texture the trees with a cocktail stick or leaf aid tool, and cut the edges to create a less solid look. Stick these on in groups, sometimes overlapping, using royal icing

(D). Let the shapes dry a little before sticking on, so that they look like little cardboard cutouts. Cut out the shapes of a few houses, and perhaps a telegraph pole, and stick onto the cake.

A Cut out the shapes for the distant hills from pale mauve flowerpaste and stick to the sides of the cake using water. The shapes need not be continuous.

B Cut out shapes for the lower hills in a variety of green shades from dark to light, plus a few in brown and yellow, and stick to the cake in the same way.

C Cut out shapes for the trees from flowerpaste in a variety of greens, using a range of different cutters. These can include Christmas trees, carnation cutters and single petal shapes.

D Stick the trees to the cake in small groups, sometimes overlapping the individual pieces. Use royal icing this time, to ensure that these smaller pieces are secure.

5 Fix the mini spots to the disc, then cover with leftover white flowerpaste. Paint with egg white, cover with a layer of sugarpaste and stipple on some diluted Bamboo and Fern droplet colour with a damp sponge. Push in the snowdrop flowers and leaves, plus shamrock leaves and one daisy flower and leaves, starting in the middle and working outwards. Slip the arrangement into place in the recess.

6 For the base arrangement, make three autumn leaves in any shape from flowerpaste coloured with Bamboo droplet colour, and when dry dust with Oak and Mustard powders. Mix up some white flowerpaste with egg white until it resembles thick royal icing. Paint this around the edges of the leaves and immediately dust with White Hologram powder to look like hoarfrost. Cover the

mini spot on the board with sugarpaste, stipple as before, then push in the flowers, leaves and a few ribbon grasses.

7 To complete, stick the matching velvet ribbon to the edge of the cake board with double-sided adhesive tape.

THE SIDE DESIGN
Have fun making the scenery, keeping the shapes simple. The houses and barns should be small and without any detail – apart, perhaps, from an occasional little chimneypot.

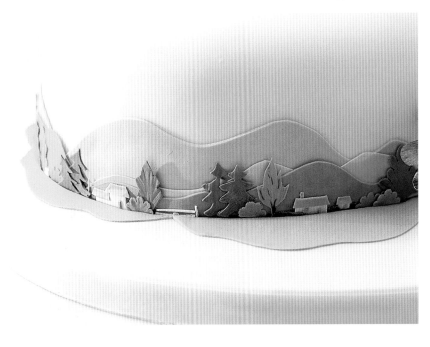

Green glory

CAKE AND DECORATION

20cm (8in) round cake and
  33cm (13in) round board,
  covered in dark green
  sugarpaste (rolled
  fondant)
Leftover white flowerpaste
  (gum paste)
Nile green florist's tape
Flowerpaste (gum paste)
  coloured with Christmas
  Green paste food colour
  (see step 2)
Heraldic Black droplet colour
Melon paste food colour
Pale green royal icing
Gelatine droplets (see
  page 11)
106cm (42in) dark green
  velvet ribbon, 1.5cm
  (⅝in) wide
Double-sided adhesive tape

SPECIAL EQUIPMENT

Flower pick
Polystyrene block
Cutter Nos 23–28
Wall tile
Roasting bag
Masking tape
Greaseproof paper
Clematis leaf templates (see
  page 126)
No. 1 piping tube (tip)

FLOWERS FOR THE TOP
ARRANGEMENT

Clematis flowers and
  leaves (see pages 24–5)

I have had the idea for this cake since painting a study of clematis and noticing how the different layers of leaves behind the flowers give a feeling of depth to the overall picture. It would not be practical to make all the leaves on wires, so I have cut simple shapes in different shades, overlapping them on the cake.

1 Put some leftover white flowerpaste (gum paste) into the flower pick and push it into a polystyrene block. Tape the clematis flowers and leaves into a group and push into the flower pick. Make a hole in the top of cake, ready for the pick. Measure and mark the positions of the leaves around the side of the cake.

2 Mix green flowerpaste in a range of shades, from light to dark. For dark shades, add some Heraldic Black droplet colour; for pale, add Melon paste food colour. Use the darker colours mainly for the larger leaves, getting lighter as they become smaller. Roll out the paste very thinly and cut out the leaves using the Nos 23–28 cutters (A). You can put in the main vein with a leaf aid tool, but this is not essential. Keep the shapes flat.

3 When the leaves are fairly dry, fix them to the cake with royal icing. Start with the large dark shapes and radiate these around the flower pick hole. Now bring in the middle sizes, moving outwards and overlapping as much as possible. The small leaves look better scattered further apart. Check that the overall design looks circular (B).

THE TOP ARRANGEMENT

Use an uneven number of clematis flowers for this arrangement, with at least one group of wired leaves for each flower stem. Make sure the leaves on the cake extend outwards beyond the flowers.

4 Position the flower arrangement on top of the cake, pushing the flower pick well down into it. Check that the leaf shapes on the cake extend outwards beyond the flower arrangement. If necessary, you can add some extra small leaves at this stage to achieve a better overall balance to the design.

A Cut out the leaves for the top of the cake from flowerpaste in a variety of greens. Use the darker colours mainly for the larger leaves.

B Stick the leaves to the cake with royal icing, starting with the larger leaves and working from the centre outwards. Scatter the smaller leaves singly.

C Fix the clematis leaf shapes to the side of the cake at the positions you measured and marked earlier. Use ten large leaves with two smaller leaves on top of each.

D Use more of the dark green sugarpaste that was used to cover the cake, this time let down with water, to pipe a snail's trail around the base.

5 Prepare the tile and trace the clematis leaf shapes from the templates onto a strip of greaseproof paper (see page 73). Pressure-pipe pale green royal icing onto the design using a No. 1 piping tube. With a wet paintbrush, pull the icing down to the point of each leaf. Finger the wet brush to a point and make marks on the icing to represent veins. When dry, fix the leaves onto the sides of the cake at the marked positions with dots of royal icing (C). In the cake shown, ten large leaves were used with two smaller leaves on top of each.

6 Pipe a snail's trail around the base of the cake using the green sugarpaste (rolled fondant) let down with water (see page 73) (D). Pipe two dots of royal icing onto each gelatine droplet directly opposite each other, then use one of the

dots to fix each droplet in place, on the points of the leaves around the side of the cake.

7 To complete, stick the matching velvet ribbon to the edge of the cake board with double-sided adhesive tape.

THE SIDE DESIGN
You will need ten large pressure-piped clematis leaves and 20 small to complete the design around the side of the cake. Gelatine droplets add the finishing touch.

Elegant blooms

These magnolias are lovely bold flowers, but I needed to scale down the size because they would have made the cake look top heavy. It was quite difficult to devise a group of plants for the base that would be in proportion with the top arrangement, so I decided on a slightly formal design of many different types of leaves.

1 Decide on the position of the flower pick and make a hole in the top of the cake in readiness. Fix a mini spot onto the perspex ruler and slide this under the cake as far as you can, where you want the base arrangement to go. Put some leftover white flowerpaste (gum paste) in the flower pick and push this into a polystyrene block.

2 Tape the magnolia stems together with florist's tape, so that you end up with three main stems going into the flower pick. You may need to strip down the lower part of one or two of the stems and perhaps take out a section of pipe cleaner if they are too bulky. Check that the height and spread of the flowers balances sensibly with the size of the cake. You can finalize the placing of the flowers later, when the arrangement has been inserted into the top of the cake.

3 For the freehand design on the top of the cake, first make the 'pebbles' from white flowerpaste. Roll a small shape and then flatten it, but also make a few that are rounded. (The number you make is your own choice, but I used 17 on the cake shown.) Using

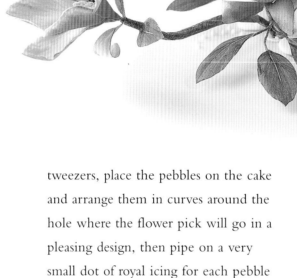

THE TOP ARRANGEMENT

Use the colour and elegance of the blooms to make this arrangement truly eye-catching. The pebbles and royal-iced dots help to keep the design flowing.

FOLIAGE FOR THE BASE ARRANGEMENT

Ivy leaves (see page 66)

Rusty-back fern
(see page 69)

Alchemilla leaves (see page 68)

Alexanders leaves (see page 63)

Rosemary sprigs (see pages 65–6)

Eucalyptus leaves (see page 66)

Ribbon grasses (see page 67)

Filler foliage

tweezers, place the pebbles on the cake and arrange them in curves around the hole where the flower pick will go in a pleasing design, then pipe on a very small dot of royal icing for each pebble

using a No. 0 piping tube (tip) and fix in place (A). Pipe some more dots of icing to continue the curves (B). Repeat the shapes of these curves in the corners of the board.

A Arrange the 'pebbles' in a pleasing design handling them with tweezers, then pipe on a dot of royal icing for each pebble and fix them in place one by one.

B Once the pebbles are fixed in position, pipe on further dots of royal icing to continue the curved lines and create an attractive overall design.

C Select leaves and grasses for the base arrangement to provide height and width, and a variety of shapes and shades of green. Adjust the arrangement with tweezers as necessary.

D Once you are satisfied with the arrangement, use tweezers to place gelatine droplets carefully on the alchemilla leaves, fixing them in position with egg white.

4 Using the lace template, pipe at least 32 pieces of lace in matching royal icing using the No. 0 piping tube. Mark out the cake side design using both templates. Pipe a snail's trail of matching sugarpaste (rolled fondant) around the cake base. Following the curved marks, pipe seven dots of royal icing at a time and push in a piece of lace on top. Do not start too close to the position of the side arrangement, to avoid breakages later.

5 For the base arrangement, cover the mini spot with a thin layer of leftover flowerpaste, paint with egg white and cover with sugarpaste. Stipple on some diluted Bamboo and Fern droplet colour (see page 71). Select leaves to give both height and width, and aim for a variety of shapes and shades. Arrange the leaves and grasses in the mini spot (C). Finally, place gelatine droplets on the alchemilla to look like dew (D).

6 Push the flower arrangement into the top of the cake and adjust if necessary. To complete, stick the matching velvet ribbon to the edge of the cake board with double-sided adhesive tape.

THE BASE ARRANGEMENT
A wide variety of leaves in different shapes, sizes and shades is arranged in a semi-formal manner to complement the simple stems of magnolia used on the top of the cake.

Pink cameo

When I happened upon some fairly small cyclamen I realized I could copy them using the same cutter as I use for roses, freesias and other blooms. Once I had made the flowers, buds and leaves I wanted to see them arranged simply as a group on this cake, for which you will need many leaves in different shades and sizes.

CAKE AND DECORATION
20cm (8in) square cake and 33cm (13in) square board, covered in champagne ivory sugarpaste (rolled fondant)
Matching royal icing
Leftover white flowerpaste (gum paste)
Bamboo and Fern droplet colours
Flowerpaste (gum paste) coloured with Christmas Green paste food colour
Gum arabic solution
Gelatine droplets (see page 11)
134cm (53in) matching velvet ribbon, 1.5cm (⅝in)
Double-sided adhesive tape

SPECIAL EQUIPMENT
Perspex disc with 3 mini spots
No. 0 piping tube (tip)
Natural sponge
Side design templates (see page 126)
Cutter Nos 40–42
Soft foam

FLOWERS FOR THE TOP ARRANGEMENT
Cyclamen flowers, buds and leaves (see pages 28–9)

1 Cut a recess in the sugarpaste (rolled fondant) in the middle of the top of the cake, the size of the perspex disc (A). Pipe dots of matching royal icing around this circle and a snail's trail of matching sugarpaste around the base of the cake, using a No. 0 piping tube (tip).

2 Fix three mini spots to the disc, then cover with leftover flowerpaste (gum paste). Paint with egg white, cover with

a layer of champagne ivory sugarpaste and trim off near to the edge of the disc. Stipple on some diluted Bamboo and Fern droplet colour with a damp sponge, fading away as you reach the edge. Starting from the centre of the disc, push in the cyclamen flowers, buds and leaves, gradually working outwards.

3 Mark out the curved shapes of the side design, using the smaller template for the corners and the larger one for the sides (B). Cut out about 40 heart shapes from green flowerpaste using the No. 40 cutter. (You may prefer to roll out and cut these, say, ten at a time.) Place each shape on soft foam and indent a vein through the centre, pressing quite hard with a leaf aid tool (C). Paint each leaf with Fern droplet colour and gum arabic solution (D), then stick it onto the side

THE TOP ARRANGEMENT
Make up the arrangement from a selection of cyclamen flowers and buds in different shades of pink and white, complemented by their pretty marbled, heart-shaped leaves.

of the cake with royal icing and lift the point away from the side with the leaf aid tool, so that it does not hang flat against the surface of the cake.

4 Add some white flowerpaste to the green to achieve a lighter tone and then cut out about 60 heart shapes using the No. 41 cutter. Work in the same way as

A Use the perspex disc to mark and cut out a recess in the sugarpaste in the middle of the top of the cake. This is where the flower arrangement will eventually be positioned.

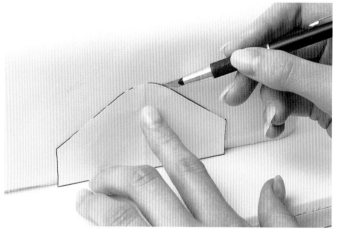

B For the side design, the smaller template is used at the corners of the cake and the larger one along the sides. Mark out the curved shapes using a scriber or similar tool.

C The leaves around the cake side are cut out in three sizes, from three shades of green flowerpaste. Indent the main vein by pressing quite hard with a leaf aid tool on soft foam.

D Paint the leaves with a mixture of Fern droplet colour and gum arabic solution, using the darkest mix for the large leaves and the palest, most dilute mix for the smallest leaves.

for the large leaves (see step 3), then paint with a more dilute mix of the Fern droplet colour and gum arabic solution. These shapes will form the next layer and an extra layer in the top part of the curves. Finish off by cutting out about 90 heart shapes from very pale green paste, using the No. 42 cutter. Paint these with the very palest mixture of Fern droplet colour and gum arabic solution. These leaves will follow the top curve and should be bent into their natural shape.

5 Pick up a gelatine droplet with tweezers and pipe on two dots of royal icing directly opposite each other, then use one of the dots to fix the droplet so that it hangs from the tip of a leaf. Place the droplets carefully wherever you can without risk of breakages to the leaves.

6 Taking great care not to damage the leaves that are sticking out, lift the flower arrangement and disc very gently and slip into the recess.

7 To complete, stick the matching velvet ribbon to the edge of the cake board with double-sided adhesive tape.

THE SIDE DESIGN
The heart-shaped leaves massed around the sides of the cake echo the shape of the cyclamen foliage used in the top arrangement. Gelatine droplets lighten the finished effect.

Cutters and templates

Some of the cutter shapes shown on these two pages are used to make more than one flower or leaf. The numbered cutters you will need are listed with the individual projects. Templates for the side designs, pressure-piped runouts, lace and freehand leaf shapes are provided on page 126.

Star cutter
1

Open rose cutter
2

Lobelia cutter for broom and scabious
3

4
Daphne cutter for mock orange blossom calyx

5
Mock orange blossom cutter

6
Stephanotis cutter for dianthus and pansy calyx

7
Large snowdrop cutter for iris and snowdrop

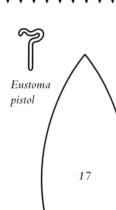
8
Large snowdrop cutter for snowdrop and shamrock

10 Rusty-back fern cutter

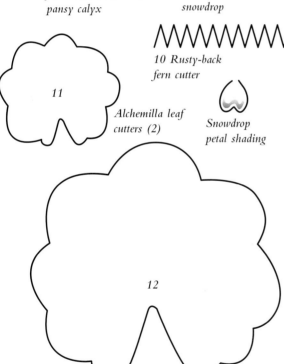
11
Alchemilla leaf cutters (2)

Snowdrop petal shading

Eustoma pistol

9
(or six points)

17

Lily cutter for tulip petal

Clematis cutter for anemone and clematis

12

Cutter for cyclamen, eustoma, freesia, gerbera, rose and sycamore seeds

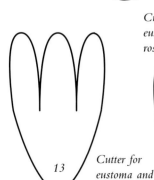
13

14
Cutter for eustoma and magnolia

Cutter for carnation, chrysanthemum, cornflower and sycamore seeds

15

16
Cutter for chrysanthemum

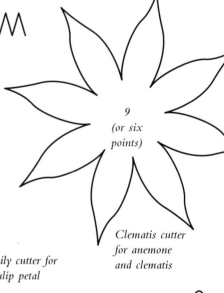
18

19

Daffodil cutters also for pansy (4)

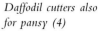

20

21

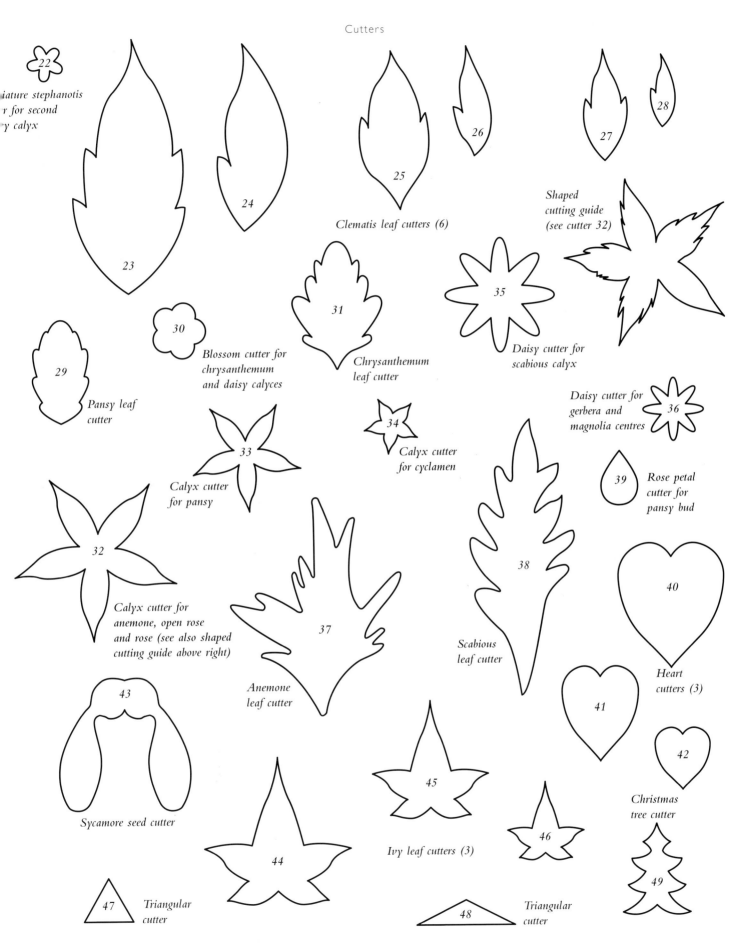

22

iature stephanotis
r for second
y calyx

23

24

25

26

27

28

Clematis leaf cutters (6)

*Shaped
cutting guide
(see cutter 32)*

31

35

30

*Blossom cutter for
chrysanthemum
and daisy calyces*

*Chrysanthemum
leaf cutter*

*Daisy cutter for
scabious calyx*

29

*Pansy leaf
cutter*

34

*Calyx cutter
for cyclamen*

*Daisy cutter for
gerbera and
magnolia centres*

36

33

*Calyx cutter
for pansy*

39

*Rose petal
cutter for
pansy bud*

32

*Calyx cutter for
anemone, open rose
and rose (see also shaped
cutting guide above right)*

38

*Scabious
leaf cutter*

40

*Heart
cutters (3)*

41

42

43

37

*Anemone
leaf cutter*

Sycamore seed cutter

45

46

*Christmas
tree cutter*

49

44

Ivy leaf cutters (3)

47

*Triangular
cutter*

48

*Triangular
cutter*

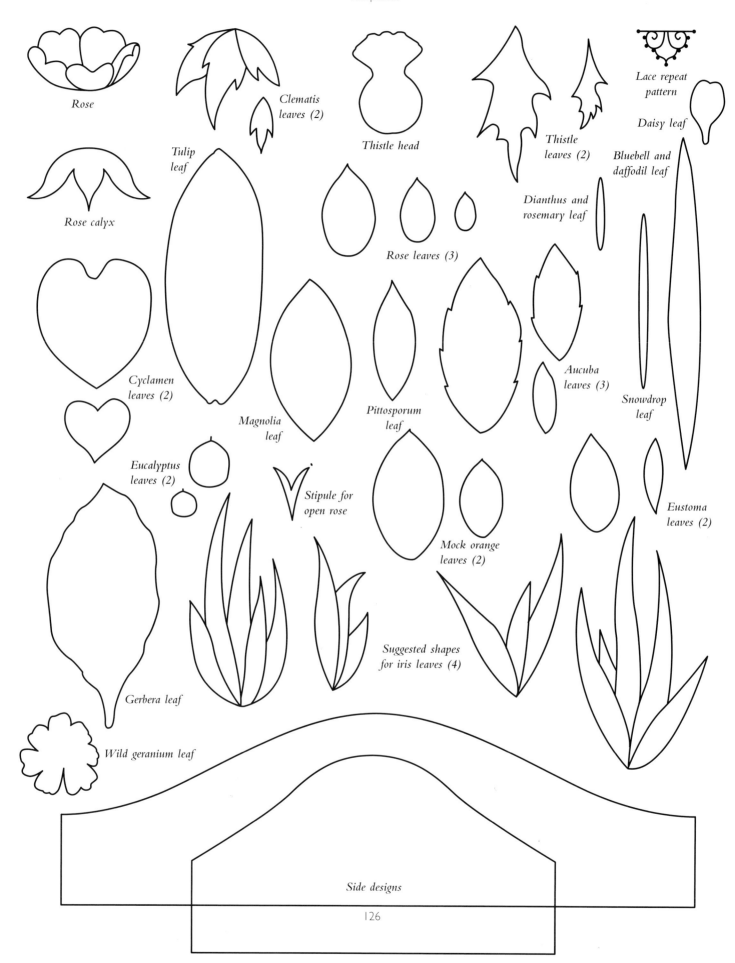

Rose

Clematis leaves (2)

Thistle head

Thistle leaves (2)

Lace repeat pattern

Daisy leaf

Tulip leaf

Bluebell and daffodil leaf

Rose calyx

Dianthus and rosemary leaf

Rose leaves (3)

Cyclamen leaves (2)

Aucuba leaves (3)

Snowdrop leaf

Magnolia leaf

Pittosporum leaf

Eucalyptus leaves (2)

Stipule for open rose

Eustoma leaves (2)

Mock orange leaves (2)

Gerbera leaf

Suggested shapes for iris leaves (4)

Wild geranium leaf

Side designs

Suppliers

UK

Cutters and equipment

AP Cutters
Treelands
Hillside Road
Bleadon
Weston-super-Mare
North Somerset
BS24 OAA
Tel/fax: +44 (0)1934 812787
(Also from all good cake decorating shops)

Culpitt Cake Art
Culpitt Ltd
Jubilee Industrial Estate
Ashington
Northumberland
NE63 8UQ
Tel: +44 (0)1670 814 545

Edable Art
1 Stanhope Close
Grange Estate
Spennymoor
Co. Durham
DL16 6LZ

Guy, Paul & Co. Ltd
Unit B4 Foundry Way
Little End Road
Eaton Socon
Cambs
PE19 3JH
Tel: +44 (0)1480 472 545

The Letter Box
94 Alfriston Gardens
Sholing
Southampton
SO19 8FU

Renshaw Scott Ltd
Crown Street
Liverpool
L8 7RF
Tel: +44 (0)151 706 8200
(Manufacturer of Regalice sugarpaste used in book)

Other distributors and retailers

Doreen Hollis
Country Cutters
Lower Trefaldu
Dingestow
Monmouth
Gwent
NP25 4BQ
Wales

Sugarflair Colours Ltd
Brunel Road
Manor Trading Estate
Benfleet
Essex
SS7 4PS
Tel: +44 (0)1286 752 891

Jan Thomas
Serendipity
26 Clos Penglyn
Pencoed
Bridgend
Mid-Glamorgan
CF35 6NX
Wales
(Supplier of ribbons)

Cakes & Co.
25 Rock Hill
Blackrock Village
Co. Dublin
Ireland
Tel: +353 (0)1 283 6544

Non-UK suppliers

Beryl's Cake Decorating
& Pastry Supplies
PO Box 1584
N. Springfield
United States
Tel: +1 800 488 2749

Creative Cutters
561 Edward Avenue
Unit 1
Richmond Hill
Ontario
L4C 9W6
Canada
Tel: +1 905 883 5638

Ediciones Ballina Codai
S.A.
Avda Cordoba 2415,
1st floor
C1120Aag
Buenos Aires
Argentina
Tel: +5411 4962 5381
Fax: +5411 4963 3751

The Cake Decorators
School of Australia
Shop 7
Port Phillip Arcade
232 Flinders Street
Melbourne
Victoria 3000
Australia
Tel: +61 (0) 3 9654 5335
Fax: +61 (0) 3 9654 5818

Choice Cake Decorating
Centre
193–197 Main Street
Lilydale 3140 Victoria
Australia

Cupid's Cake Decorations
2/90 Belford Street
Broadmeadow
New South Wales 2292
Australia
Tel: +61 (0) 2 4962 1884
Fax: +61 (0) 2 4961 6594

Rosemary Scalzi
The Major Cake
Decorating Supplies
900 Albany Highway
East Victoria Park
Western Australia 6101

Suzy Q Cake Decorating
Centre
Shop 4
372 Keilor Road
Niddrie
Victoria 3042
Australia

The Cake Decorating Shop
MacQuarie Street
4 Cascade Raod
South Hobart
7004 Tasmania

First published in 2002 by Murdoch Books UK Ltd
Merehurst is an imprint of Murdoch Books UK Ltd

Flower designs Copyright © 2002 Alison Procter

Text, photographs and illustrations copyright ©
2002 Murdoch Books UK Ltd

ISBN 1 85391 934 9
A catalogue record of this book is available
from the British Library.

Commissioning Editor: Barbara Croxford
Project Editor: Sarah Widdicombe
Design: Alyson Kyles
Photography: Michael Dannenberg

CEO: Robert Oerton
Publisher: Catie Ziller
Production Manager: Lucy Byrne
International Sales Director: Kevin Lagden

Colour separation by Colourscan, Singapore
Printed and bound by Tien Wah Press, Singapore

1st Paperback Edition Published
in April 2005 by A.P.Cutters
Re-printed Oct 2006
4th Re-print May 2009 by A.P.Cutters.

Text, Photographs and illustrations
copyright © 2005 A.P.Cutters

ISBN 0-9525848-1-6

A.P.Cutters,
"Treelands",
Hillside Road,
BLEADON.
Weston-super-Mare.
North Somerset BS24 OAA.
UK.

Tel/Fax: +44 (0) 1934 812787.

e-mail tony.procter@tesco.net

Acknowledgements

My special thanks to Hugh and Maureen Blakemore, for making the cutters, and to John and Elizabeth Wright. Also my thanks to Ann Cornwell, Rosemary McDonald and Yvonne Radford.

Also to Landy Kober of Choice Cake Decorating Centre, without whose gift of the best non-stick mat I have ever used the job of rolling out all the sugarpaste would have been much more difficult. And finally, many thanks for the cheerful support of my Wednesday Girls, who so valiantly tried out my failures and successes.

Index

Note: The following flowers are reproduced larger than actual size: pp 10, 15, 17, 19, 21, 23, 25, 29, 33, 47, 49, 53, 55, 57. All the flowers and cakes in this book are the original work of the author. Flowerpaste was used to make all flowers and foliage.